DETROIT
DREAM CARS

JOHN HEILIG

MBI Publishing Company

First published in 2001 by MBI Publishing Company, Galtier Plaza, Suite 200, 380 Jackson St., St. Paul, MN 55101-3885, USA

MBI Publishing Company books are also available at discounts in bulk quantity for industrial or sales-promotional use. For details write to Special Sales Manager at Motorbooks International Wholesalers & Distributors, Galtier Plaza, Suite 200, 380 Jackson St., St. Paul, MN 55101-3885, USA

On the front cover: Three great dream cars from the past and present, from the top: the 1938 Buick Y-Job, the 1954 Buick Wildcat II, and the 1998 Plymouth Pronto Spyder.

On the frontispiece: The streamlined 1987 Pontiac Pursuit.

On the title page: The Chevrolet XP-700. This car began as a 1960 Corvette and was customized for GM executive Bill Mitchell.

On the back cover: A quartet of classic dream cars, including the Mustang I, Ford X-100, Chrysler Phaeton, and AMC AMX/2.

Library of Congress Cataloging-in-Publication Data Available

ISBN 0-7603-0838-1

Edited by Keith Mathiowetz
Designed by Bruce Leckie

Printed in the United States of America

Contents

Acknowledgments

I thank the following people for their assistance in the creation of this book:

Bob Ashton. I've never met Bob, but he auctioned off some dream car press kits and information on eBay that were invaluable.

Jim and Bonnie Fegler. This couple runs an antique and collectibles store in Allentown, Pennsylvania. Every book project I've had owes something to them, primarily for ads. In this book, they supplied the very rare photo of the bronze LeSabre, as well as two ads using dream cars.

Wayne Cherry, vice president of design at General Motors. I literally grabbed Wayne at the 2000 New York Auto Show and picked his brain for a few minutes. His answers were forthright and to the point.

Pam Clark, of the Oldsmobile History Center. Pam searched the archives for photographs that many people thought had disappeared.

Edward R. Golden, design director of Ford's Truck Vehicle Center. He led me to the right people at Ford.

Larry Gustin of Buick. Larry fanned the flames of an interest in dream and concept cars, then introduced me to Bill Porter, who is one of the most knowledgeable designers I have ever met. To Larry goes thanks for all the Buick information and for setting up the "Field of Dreams" photo at Grand Traverse Resort.

John Herlitz, Tom Gale and others at Daimler Chrysler. I thank these people for their knowledge, talent, and willingness to talk about their craft.

Harvey Ledesma. He shepherded the three Firebirds to the Burn Foundation Concours d'Elegance of the Eastern United States and tolerated all my dumb questions and requests for photos.

Mike Mueller, an old friend, for the Ford GT 90 photos. We stood goggle-eyed together at that unveiling.

Vince Muniga of Oldsmobile, former PR director for the GM Design Center. He remembered a lot and led me to the right people.

Art Ponder, DaimlerChrysler Historical Center, for all the great historical Chrysler Corporation photos.

Bill Porter, formerly of Buick. I first met Bill when he was still at Buick. He has since retired. He conducted a class in a walkaround around the Buick dream cars at Detroit's Eyes on Classic Design car show, then carefully edited an article with shared bylines (I just wrote it; he supplied the comments).

Ken Ruddock, automotive advertising historian. Ken and I worked together for a brief time, and he supplied many manufacturers' brochures from the past on dream cars.

Greg Wallace, Cadillac History Center, for historical Cadilllac photos and editorial assistance.

As with all other projects, I could not have completed this one without the support and love of my wife Florence and our three daughters, three sons-in-law, and one grandson, who appeared about halfway along in the project. Now *there's* a great design.

—*John Heilig*

Introduction

In the beginning there was Harley Earl, and what Earl began has been with us for more than 65 years. True, dream cars/concept cars/idea cars would have been with us even if there was no Harley Earl, and in reality some manufacturers had versions of concept cars before Earl began his magic at General Motors, but still, Earl is considered the father of the idea.

It was Earl's Buick Y-Job of 1938 that is generally credited with being the first American dream car. It was unique. It was aerodynamic in an era when aerodynamics was a pragmatic science. It was stylish in an era of Duesenbergs and V-12 Lincolns and Cadillacs. It had gadgets and features available nowhere else (at the time) but, that would appear on future cars.

Before the Y-Job there was the Auburn Cabin Speedster, which was supposed to go into production but didn't quite make it. Earl's 1933 Cadillac V-16 Aero-Dynamic Coupe, shown at the Chicago World's Fair, also precedes the Y-Job, but it *did* go into production, albeit low volume.

Dream cars usually give us a glimpse of the future. It may be a long look, as with the Y-Job or Ford Mustang I, or it may be a fleeting glance, as with the Cadillac Cyclone. In some cases, however, the look is backward, as with the Plymouth Prowler and Chrysler PT Cruiser.

In all cases, dream cars are designed to quicken our pulses and make us want to buy whatever that manufacturer is offering today, with the tacit understanding that what's in today's cars is almost the same as the dream cars.

That's why dream cars are usually presented to the public at automobile shows around the country and the world. Automobile shows are fantasies in themselves. The people who attend them may not really be shopping for a new car, but they're shopping for an idea. Or, they may simply be looking for entertainment. And this is where the dream cars come in.

Volkswagen introduced its New Beetle concept car at an auto show to gauge public reaction. Dodge showed the Viper and the Copperhead to determine if there would be sufficient public interest if it offered either of those cars for sale. The Viper won. Similarly, Plymouth tested the waters with its Prowler, Chrysler with the PT Cruiser, and Ford with the new Thunderbird.

Many dream cars, though, have no chance of ever reaching production. Some have exotic powerplants that would be difficult or impossible to implement in production. Some have exotic powerplants that *still* haven't been invented. Some are used as platforms for new styling technologies, or new paint schemes, or new interior design theories. Some push the styling envelope to see how much it will stretch. Some stretch it far beyond the practical. In any case, dream cars serve a purpose, whether it's to entertain, to educate, to test market, or to serve as a test bed.

Harley Earl—*nobody* called him Harley; it was *always* Mister Earl or Misterl—was born in Los Angeles in 1893. His father owned the Earl Automotive Works, a company that built custom-designed coach-built bodies for luxury automobiles. When Don Lee of Don Lee Cadillac bought the Earl Automotive Works in 1919, Harley went with the company as chief designer.

Soon, Earl's designs were reaching the East Coast auto shows, where they attracted the attention of Alfred Sloan and the Fisher brothers of General Motors. In December 1925, Larry Fisher, who was president of the Cadillac division, called Earl in Hollywood. Fisher explained that the GM designers were working on a plan for a less expensive companion car to the Cadillac. Would Earl be interested in submitting a design?

Earl spent the first three months of 1926 in Detroit working on his designs. He offered Fisher four full-size and painted clay models to examine: a runabout roadster, a coupe, a four-door sedan, and a touring car. All were inspired by the Hispano-Suiza, one of Earl's favorite cars. His design was accepted immediately for what would be the first LaSalle.

Earl returned to California, but received another call from Sloan in June 1927, offering him the opportunity to head up what would be called the Art and Colour Section. He was to direct "general production body design and conduct research and development programs in special car design," according to Sloan. In 1937, the name of the division was changed from Art and Colour to General Motors Styling. From 1927 to 1958, Earl was *the* designer at General Motors and was instrumental in creating the greatest dream cars ever to hit the show circuit.

Succeeding Earl at GM in 1959 was Bill Mitchell, who started working in the Cadillac studio in 1935. A year later he was in charge. Mitchell's watershed car was the 1938 Sixty Special. Originally intended to be a LaSalle with a narrow vertical grille, the finished product wore a wider grille, had two-piece doors, and narrow chrome frames around the side windows. Although it was a four-door sedan, it had the trunk of a coupe. Mitchell added his trademark "creased pants" windsplits on the fender tops.

Michael Lamm and David Holls wrote, in *A Century of Automotive Style*:

> In commanding the largest army of automobile stylists in the world, Mitchell carried over quite a few traits he'd learned from Harley Earl. He had Earl's flair down pat: the flamboyance, showmanship, confidence and pugnacity. Yet Mitchell differed in his fundamental design philosophy. His disagreement wasn't so much with Earl's credo of "lower, longer, wider," but Mitchell's idea of good design focused more on the overall shape of the car; the underlying form. Earl spent time on form, too, but he frosted it with a lot of chrome and ornamentation. Mitchell's cars hit the eyes as one piece, one homogeneous whole, whereas Earl's moved the viewer's eye from a dominant focal point to secondary lines and patches— from a grille, say, or the entire front end to details like speed streaks or fins and then, finally, to the overall shape of the body. Form was Earl's canvas, and he pasted over it like a collage. With Mitchell, form was the entire picture.

Automotive stylist Virgil Max Exner endured basic training under Earl, as did many designers of the era. Born in 1909 in Ann Arbor, Michigan, Exner started working at a company called Allied Artists in South Bend, Indiana, drawing Studebaker cars and trucks for brochures and catalogs.

Exner heard that GM was looking for designers in 1934, drove to Detroit, interviewed with Howard O'Leary, and landed a job in the Pontiac studio under Franklin Q. Hershey. When Hershey transferred to Opel in 1937, Exner replaced him at Pontiac.

Raymond Loewy was designing cars for Studebaker and lured Exner back, first to New York and then to South Bend. Exner and Loewy had a falling out over the design of the 1947 Studebaker. Loewy's design was rejected; Exner's,

which he and clay modeler Frank Ahlroth developed in Exner's basement, was accepted. Loewy fired Exner, Studebaker fired Loewy, and Studebaker hired Exner. Roy E. Cole, Studebaker's chief engineer, was nearing retirement and started looking for greener pastures for his favorite designer. He thought he found Exner a job at Ford, but when that didn't materialize, he called K. T. Keller at Chrysler, who hired Exner in 1949.

As design director and, later, vice president of design, Exner modernized the Chrysler design department. His "Forward Look" cars of 1955 may well have inspired Earl to fin mania, culminating in the excesses of the 1959 Cadillac. Exner suffered a heart attack in 1956 that led to his early retirement. Elwood Engel replaced him.

Dick Teague's life was fashioned by the automobile. Born in 1923 in Los Angeles, he became a child movie actor until an auto accident cost him an eye, a couple of teeth, and a broken jaw. An early hot-rodder, he became an aircraft illustrator during World War II, but spent most of his time drawing cars.

In 1948, Teague began working for Franklin Hershey at GM, drawing headlights and trim pieces. He moved to Cadillac, then left GM and returned to California. Hershey, meanwhile, had moved on to Packard and offered Teague the chief stylist's job in 1951. When Hershey went to Ford, Teague became styling director.

Teague left for Chrysler in 1956, and went to American Motors in 1959 under Ed Anderson, for whom he had worked at GM. When Anderson left AMC in 1961, Teague was named styling director. He became vice president of design in 1964 and stayed with AMC until 1983.

Franklin Quick Hershey (he was named after an uncle) was born in Detroit to a family of "early automobilists" in 1907. They moved to California when his mother became enchanted with the state through advertisements.

After studying geology with the full intention of becoming a forest ranger, Hershey landed a job with Walter M. Murphy Co., Coachbuilders, in 1928.

"I caught on right away," Hershey wrote in *Automobile Quarterly*. "My first design was for a Mercedes town car, then I did a Rolls-Royce." In three years he produced designs for 30 custom cars.

Murphy closed in 1932 and Hershey moved to Hudson. After three months he received a call from Howard O'Leary, who was assistant director of the Art and Colour Section at GM. Hershey was sent to the Pontiac studio and in two weeks came up with a new design for the 1933 eight-cylinder car. One of his innovations was the "silver streak" that became Pontiac's trademark until well after World War II.

After stops at Buick and Opel, Hershey was put in charge of the Advanced Design Studio at GM. After World War II, he was temporarily assigned to Cadillac where (he claimed) he had the idea to add fins to the rear fenders.

He left Cadillac and established his own design firm in New Mexico, but he returned to Detroit after the Korean War to work for Packard. In 1952 he moved to Ford as director of car and truck styling. In that position he promoted the introduction of the 1954 Thunderbird.

Bill Mitchell was succeeded by Irv Rybicki, who was succeeded by Chuck Jordan, who was succeeded by Wayne Cherry. Cherry, at the 2000 New York International Automobile Show, gave his opinions of the purpose of dream cars:

> I think dream cars—concept vehicles—have been used for many things over history. I think in many cases they have evolved, in some cases, from pure fantasy of what might be, into serious indications of what's actually coming. Certainly, with the vehicles we're showing here [six dream cars at the 2000 NYIAS], they've come right out of our development process, so from a design perspective, we're extremely happy because we're actually showing the work that's going on inside GM right now as opposed to dreaming up dream cars or trucks.

Harley Earl exerted great influence over the vehicles that emerged from GM during his tenure. Does Cherry have the same influence? "It's a different world," he answered.

At Ford, the designers who worked for Edsel Ford—Bob Gregoire, Homer LaGassey—saw their studios eventually taken over by the likes of Gene Bordinat and Jack Telnack, as there was no single guiding light like Earl at GM. Chrysler's renaissance in recent years has been under the guidance of Tom Gale and John Herlitz, but before

them there was the genius Virgil Exner. The independents—Brooks Stevens, Raymond Loewy—and the Italian design houses of Ghia, Bertone, and Pininfarina have always stood ready to present us with superbly styled vehicles.

Tom Gale (executive vice president of product strategy and design at DaimlerChrysler at the time this book was written) said in an interview with Jim Mateja of the *Chicago Tribune* that Chrysler's recent splurge of concept and dream cars was the result of not having a lot of new products in the showrooms to brag about. "For too long we simply reinvented what we had done in the past," Gale said. "I told the staff I wanted to stop being reactive to automotive styling, get off the defensive, and get on the offensive. I told my people that good design adds value faster than it adds cost. So I took one-third of the staff and told them to work on concepts."

There were some losers—like the Plymouth Voyager II that split in half to form two vehicles, but there were also winners—like the Dodge Viper and Plymouth Prowler. "We wanted to come up with the unexpected to get attention," Gale added. "We listen to what people say about the concepts and watch our mail. When the Viper appeared at auto shows, people started sending us blank checks. That's being earnest about a car. You listen at auto shows and read your mail, and it's easy to tell when people have passion and are serious about a vehicle more so than when you conduct formal research and ask people what they want in the future and find they can't verbalize."

Attention to concept and dream cars pays off. "In the past we were the laggard of the industry in revenue generated per vehicle and now we have the highest revenue per vehicle of any of our domestic competitors," Gale said.

At last count, there were more than 250 cars that qualified as dream cars from American manufacturers. That number is increasing every year as new design theories are tested and new technologies advanced. So while this volume presents a snapshot in time and a look at what has come before, be aware that tomorrow there will be a whole new collection to excite our senses and quicken our heartbeats.

Primarily because of space limitations, several vehicles had to be left out of this volume. We also stopped counting at the end of the 1999 "model year" (dream cars by definition have no strict model year designation).

CHAPTER 1

Buick

For many years, Buick was the General Motors division that led the way in styling. Harley Earl and his associates worked their magic on Buick chassis, creating some of the most creative, beautiful, and outlandish automobiles ever seen. While his background was with Cadillac, his greatest creations were at Buick, beginning with the Y-Job, an enormous two-seater convertible that predicted many styling trends of the future. Many of the people who followed Earl also worked with Buicks, most notably Ned Nickles, Homer LaGassey, Bill Porter, Wayne Kady, Phil Garcia, and Steve Pastiner.

Here is the story of the seminal Y-Job and its successors.

1939 Y-Job

Harley Earl began work on the Y-Job in 1938 and finished it in late 1939. The public saw it for the first time a year later. The name for the Y-Job came from fighter planes; GM designers claimed that the letter "Y" was used to designate new fighter planes being developed by the aircraft industry. "Y" was chosen for experimental cars and grew to become a term of endearment in the GM design studios. Earl also tended to use "job" to refer to his project cars.

Although Earl is credited with the design, he only directed it. According to Chuck Jordan, who would eventually become vice president of design at GM, Earl couldn't draw. He did, however, have an innate sense of design and could direct subtle changes that could make all the difference in a design. The actual drawing and modeling of the Y-Job was the responsibility of George Snyder.

The Y-Job was a two-passenger convertible, almost 20 feet long, based on a standard 1937 Buick chassis that was modified by Charlie Chayne, Buick's chief engineer. With a fuselage and fenders that approached a teardrop shape, the Y-Job was a clear departure from most of the other cars of the 1930s. Among the other unique features were disappearing headlamps, flush door handles, power windows, finned drum brakes, a power-operated disappearing convertible top, and no running boards. The Y-Job rode on 13-inch wheels and tires, about 3 inches smaller than what most cars of the era were using.

Earl's goal was to make cars lower and longer, "Because my sense of proportion tells me that oblongs are more attractive than squares." The Y-Job fit that description.

Autocar commented on the dash of the Y-Job, "Also noteworthy is an unusual arrangement of the instrument panel, with a radio unit inset at the middle and its controls mounted on top. Speedometer and gauges are placed in front of the steering wheel with the large speedometer dial high on the panel for best visibility. Hand throttle, ignition switch, and control switches for automatic hood, window regulators, heater and defroster, windscreen wipers, [hood] and [trunk] locks, and lamps are grouped in an orderly way around the radio unit."

Earl kept the Y-Job as his own personal transportation. He would drive it to clubs around the Detroit area to impress the clubs' members. Later, wraparound bumpers and a Hydra-Matic transmission were added.

In 1995, Buick assembled all its dream cars on a field in Grand Traverse, Michigan, which begged the title "Field of Dreams." It was only the second time all the cars had been together in one location.
Buick Public Relations

1951 XP-300

Buick had two 1951 dream cars, the XP-300 and the LeSabre. Harley Earl and Charles Chayne, vice president of engineering for GM, disagreed on the approach to these cars, prompting Earl to tell Chayne, "Okay, you do your car and I'll do mine." The XP-300 was Chayne's and the LeSabre became Earl's. Of course, Earl supplied the stylists for both cars and Chayne supplied the engineers, but the onus for each rested on different shoulders.

Chayne once complained that, "The stylists always want to build cars very low and never seem to understand that underneath the body must be certain things that make the car go and stop." The XP-300 was extremely low-slung when compared with contemporary cars. It stood only 39 inches tall at the cowl and 53.4 inches tall with the top up. It was also about 5 inches thicker through the body than the LeSabre and it was more conservatively styled, although Chayne's group added their own jet fighter motifs. The XP-300 had a softer, blunter nose and vestigial fins in the rear, complete with a jet-engine "exhaust." The front fenders extended through the doors, as in the Y-Job, and continued all the way back to the rear bumper.

This car had an all-aluminum body and a two-piece trunk that could be opened from either side, with piano hinges in the middle. The doors had hydraulically operated steel bars that slid into position when they were closed. Automatic jacks could be used to help repair any flat tires.

The XP-300 also had four-wheel disc brakes that were cooled by forced air.

The XP-300 was powered by a 215-cubic-inch (3.5-liter) V-8 that produced 335 horsepower on a mixture of premium gasoline and methanol. There were two fuel tanks, one for gasoline and one for alcohol, in the rear fenders. Top speed was in the neighborhood of 140 miles per hour.

The interior featured lots of instruments, as one might expect from an engineer. Chayne even included gauges for horsepower output and transmission oil level.

1951 LeSabre

In 1955, *Motor Life* called the LeSabre the most famous of all dream cars. The LeSabre was credited with introducing numerous ideas into production, including bumpers with chrome nacelles, the wraparound windshield, the Buick side spear, and tailfins.

Like the XP-300, the LeSabre was powered by a 215-cubic-inch V-8 that developed more than 300 horsepower. It was supercharged with a 10:1 compression ratio and burned a combination of standard premium fuel and methanol that would cut in after 1/4 throttle opening. Fuel was carried in two 20-gallon special rubberized cells in the rear fenders, again like the XP-300. The LeSabre also had four-wheel disc brakes.

The LeSabre was built on a 115-inch wheelbase and was 200 inches long overall, 76.75 inches wide at the front,

Buick's Y-Job was a two-passenger convertible, almost 20 feet long, that was based on a standard 1937 Buick chassis. The fuselage and fenders approached a teardrop shape. Among the other unique features were disappearing headlamps, flush door handles, power windows, finned drum brakes, a power-operated disappearing convertible top, and no running boards. *John Heilig*

The XP-300 was designed under the guidance of Buick chief enginer Charles Chayne. It was extremely low-slung when compared with contemporary cars and stood only 39 inches tall at the cowl and 53.4 inches tall with the top up. This car had an all-aluminum body and a two-piece trunk that could be opened from either side, with "piano" hinges in the middle. *John Heilig*

and 72.5 inches wide at the rear. It was 36.25 inches to the top of the cowl and 50 inches to the top of the raised roof. Because it was viewed as a test bed, the LeSabre carried a full complement of instruments, including an altimeter, compass, oil temperature and oil level gauges, tachometer, speedometer, and others. Built-in hydraulic jacks helped the driver repair any flats. A rain sensor was located between the seats. If the car was parked with the top down and a drop of rain fell on the sensor, the top would automatically raise.

Former Buick designer Bill Porter once said, "Many of us who are over 50 can remember opening the pages of *Life* magazine in 1951 and seeing a full-page spread of this sensational pale copper car (it was later repainted its present light metallic blue) photographed against a black background. What a knockout! There was the future, there was heaven, there was everything!"

1953 Wildcat I

Designed by Ned Nickles, the first Wildcat was a white fiberglass creation that lent many of its innovations to future Buick designs. For example, the Wildcat I had a "waterfall" grille that has been used by Buick through the 1990s, bullet bumper overriders, and a wraparound windshield.

Wildcat I was a three-seat convertible that was powered by a stock 188-horsepower V-8 engine coupled to a Twin Turbine Dynaflow automatic transmission. Its purpose was to test the possibility of using fiberglass in automobile construction. As such, the styling was relatively conservative, with an almost-normal Buick profile. A few changes were notable. For one, the traditional Buick portholes were moved from the sides of the fenders to the tops. And the wheel discs remained stationary while the wheels revolved around them.

The Wildcat I contributed the grille and twin "Dagmars" (large bumper protectors shaped somewhat like breasts and named after the television star of the same name) to the production cars of 1955. In the rear were small fins and exhaust ports that exited through the body. The Wildcat I was built on a 114-inch wheelbase and was 192 inches long overall. Although the Wildcat I was originally pale green, it has been repainted white. Inside, the original pale-green leather upholstery remains.

Motor Life called the LeSabre the most famous of all dream cars. It was credited with introducing numerous ideas into production, including: bumpers with chrome nacelles, the wraparound windshield, the Buick side spear, and tailfins. Because it was viewed as a test bed, LeSabre carried a full complement of instruments, including an altimeter, compass, oil temperature and oil level gauges, tachometer, speedometer, and others. Built-in hydraulic jacks helped the driver repair any flats. A rain sensor was located between the seats. *John Heilig*

Wildcat I was a three-seat convertible that was designed by Ned Nickles. It was powered by a stock 188 horsepower V-8 engine coupled to a Twin Turbine Dynaflow automatic transmission. Its purpose was to test the possibility of using fiberglass in automobile construction. As such, the styling was relatively conservative, with an almost-normal Buick profile, although the car contributed the grille and twin "Dagmars" to 1955 production cars. **Buick Public Relations**

1954 Landau

The Landau was built on the same chassis used for the Super and Roadmaster, with a 127-inch wheelbase. The front half of the car was basically stock, but the rear was designed to resemble a chauffeur-driven limousine. The driver's compartment was finished in black leather and had a sliding glass divider between it and the passenger compartment. In the rear, the seats were upholstered in ivory leather, with mouton carpeting to highlight the sumptuousness. There was a bar installed in the armrest between the two rear seats. The trunk was raised for two reasons. First, it held more luggage than the standard Buick, and second, the rear part of the hood would fold flat into the deck if the passengers wanted open-air motoring.

1954 Wildcat II

Homer LaGassey called the Wildcat II "a real freak." Ned Nickles heavily influenced this car. Bill Porter said, "It was a maverick and the first of what I would call the show car glitz. I worked on a lot of the trim. I worked on the grille, which showed up on the 1955 production model. We had Dayton wire wheels that we picked up at $500 apiece. When you set this car alongside anything that General

Wildcat III was a red two-door four-passenger fiberglass convertible with red leather interior. It had a sloping beltline with completely exposed rear wheels. The hood sloped toward the front of the car, increasing immediate forward vision. *Buick Public Relations*

Motors had at the time, it was so different. A lot of the themes for this car were carried on the 1954 Skylark, which was the Buick Century carried to the extreme."

Wildcat II was a direct evolution of the XP-300. It was much smaller than anything Buick was producing at the time and was 35.3 inches tall at the cowl. It shared many chassis components with the early Chevrolet Corvette. Unlike the Corvette, though, Wildcat II had exposed front wheel arches—lined in chrome—with Kelsey-Hayes chrome wire wheels. The freestanding headlamps were similar to those Virgil Exner used with the 1961 Chrysler Imperial. Wildcat II also had an extremely raked wraparound windshield that Porter called "a real knee-knocker for a person getting in or out of the car." The interior had knee bolsters under the dash that were placed there for safety considerations. Upholstery matched the outside body color, which was originally metallic blue.

The traditional Buick portholes were moved from the fenders to the sides of the hood form. At the rear, the deck was similar to that of the early Corvette, with a small fin that was later used on the 1955 Skylark. The exhaust pipes exited through openings in the lower rear body surface.

Porter called the Wildcat II "a very interesting car for Buick at this time because Buick was not building any small

The interior of the Wildcat II had knee bolsters under the dash for safety purposes. At the rear, the deck was similar to that of the early Corvette, with a small fin that was later used on the 1955 Skylark. Exhaust pipes exited through openings in the lower rear body surface. Bill Porter called the Wildcat II "a very interesting car for Buick at this time because Buick was not building any small hot cars." *John Heilig*

Among the futuristic features of the Centurion's interior was a gear selector that was a dial in the center of the steering wheel. The steering wheel itself was cantilevered on a long arm that extended from a central pod. Instrumentation included a speedometer disc in front of the driver with a stationary needle and a rotating number disc that moved larger numbers past the needle as speeds increased. *John Heilig*

hot cars. Yet the fact that the Wildcat II was done at all suggests that Buick's designers were dying to try their hand at that genre. Buick's management never made their feelings known."

1955 Wildcat III

Homer LaGassey said he felt more responsible for the Wildcat III than any other car. Wildcat III was a red two-door four-passenger fiberglass convertible with a red leather interior. It had a sloping beltline and the rear wheels were completely exposed. The hood sloped toward the front of the car, increasing immediate forward vision. The fine-screen grille was wide and low and the parking and directional lights were housed in the bumper "bombs." The engine was a 280-horsepower V-8.

1956 Centurion

Bill Porter calls the 1956 Centurion "one of the incredible fantasies of the mid-fifties." This car was announced in 1956 and shown as a Motorama car at the Waldorf-Astoria Hotel in New York. The Buick staff designed it; Ned Nickles was the head designer. Pete Roegner did some of the

early drawings on the car when he was a summer intern. Even Chuck Jordan worked on the car.

Among the futuristic features of the interior was a gear selector that wasn't a lever but a dial in the center of the steering wheel. The steering wheel itself was cantilevered on a long arm that extended from a central pod. Instrumentation included a speedometer disc in front of the driver with a stationary needle and a rotating number disc that moved larger numbers past the needle as speed increased. In the center of the dash was an early black-and-white television screen that replaced the rearview mirror. A camera was located in the tail cone to show rear traffic.

As with many early GM dream cars, the top was a clear canopy like a fighter plane. The Centurion's canopy was constructed of glass, however. Porter added that the compound bends in the Centurion would not have been practical in a production car, although they were feasible for prototypes.

Porter added that many designers of the era felt that this was a well-proportioned car. One unique feature was fenders that were higher than the hood, which was a fresh idea in the 1950s.

1958 XP-75

This was a two-passenger coupe with twin white leather bucket seats. It was hand-built by Pininfarina in Turin, Italy. Its winglike rear fins became a 1959 Buick styling feature and its sculpted metal side treatment a hallmark of the 1960 Buick line. Features included power windows, air conditioning, paddle-type door releases, floor-mounted transmission lever, vertically indicating radio, and a specially designed steering wheel. The engine was a 348-cubic-inch V-8. The car was featured in GM's Milestone Parade in 1958.

1963 Riviera Silver Arrow

This car was Buick's answer to the "Sheer Look" introduced by Frigidaire on its 1959 refrigerators. The lines of this car were square and crisp-edged. The Silver Arrow was the work of Bill Mitchell, the new vice president of design at GM. The car was Mitchell's custom personal lowered 1963 Riviera, which was 2 to 3 inches shorter and 5 to 6 inches lower than the stock car. It was Mitchell's vision of what a Rolls-Royce would look like if it was crossed with a Ferrari. Bill Porter said of the Riviera Silver Arrow, "It has the very sheer, crisp, and dignified top of a Rolls-Royce, but it also has the rakish proportions of a Ferrari."

"Buick was fortunate to get the Riv," Porter continued. "The Riviera never said 'Buick' on it. It was always badged 'Riviera.' It is to Buick what Corvette has always been to Chevrolet. It's Buick's special high-style car. It was a new concept: the first practical personal four-passenger car. A few years later the Mustang would take that same concept and offer it for $2,000 less and, of course, it was one of the runaway best-sellers of the decade. This car is very important for Buick, and it represents Bill Mitchell's personal interpretation of the Riviera."

Some of the design elements were subtle. For example, Mitchell used different shades of silver paint on the top and side of the car in order to accent the faceted shape. The color was also shaded darker down and out again at the wheel.

1983 Questor

This car was developed at the suggestion of Delco Electronics, which was looking for a vehicle to showcase the company's electronic products. It has no engine; it's simply a body shell on a body-integral frame. Steve Pastiner designed the exterior, based on sketches by Ben Salvador. William C. Quan did the interior. He later went on to Boeing and instrumentation design.

XP-75 was a two-passenger coupe with twin white leather bucket seats. It was hand-built by Pininfarina in Turin, Italy. Its wing-like rear fins became a 1959 Buick styling feature and its sculpted metal side treatment a hallmark of the 1960 Buick line. *Buick Public Relations*

The Buick Riviera Silver Arrow was Buick's answer to the "Sheer Look" introduced by Frigidare on its 1959 refrigerators. Lines of this car were square and crisp-edged. The car was Bill Mitchell's custom personal, a lowered 1963 Riviera, which was two to three inches shorter and five to six inches lower than the stock car and was his interpretation of what a Rolls-Royce would look like if it was crossed with a Ferrari. *John Heilig*

The Questor had all the electronic innovations of the era, including a CRT screen in the center of the dash. It also had a telephone, navigation system with its own map, and controls in the steering wheel. The Questor used a laser-key entry that was like a modern remote keyless entry. The laser key would not only lock and unlock the doors, it would also operate jacks that would raise the car 6 inches for easier entry, would turn on the on-board systems, and return everything to the driver's preferred settings.

The individual bucket seats in the Questor were segmented, and each part was adjustable to fit the occupant's preferred riding position.

Questor was developed at the suggestion of Delco Electronics and has no engine; it's simply a body shell on a body integral frame. Questor had all the electronic innovations of the era, including a CRT screen in the center of the dash. It also had a telephone, navigation system with its own map, and controls in the steering wheel. *John Heilig*

Lucerne was originally designed as a coupe in 1988 but was reworked in 1991 as a convertible. As a coupe, it was very much related to the contemporary Riviera in that it was a big, elegant four-passenger two-door car. The overall length was 22 inches longer than Riviera's, while the wheelbase was only six inches longer, creating longer overhangs. *John Heilig*

1985 Wildcat

The latest Wildcat was intended to be a pace car for the CART PPG Championship series. It never was used as a pace car because the suspension was not developed to the point where it would feel safe on a track at 155 miles per hour. It was mainly a paint-and-materials technology car for PPG, but it was also a showcase for Buick's racing engine. In fact, the engine sat exposed at the rear of the car. Bill Porter calls it "the RoboCop approach to car design—part animal, part machine. The long sexy surfaces are clearly very fluid, very aerodynamic. Pieces and parts of the machinery are allowed to show through the skin and actually become part of the surface to let you know that there's something very heavy going on underneath this beautiful skin."

Wayne Katy, who worked in the Buick design studio for a while, said he felt there was no reason to hide the mechanical parts of a car. "This sort of android idea is still around," Katy said. "How can you make the mechanical innards of a vehicle manifest—more than just implied—in very beautiful aerodynamic skins?"

The latest Wildcat was intended to be a pace car for the CART PPG Championship series. It never was used as a pace car because the suspension was not developed to the point where it would feel safe on a track at 155 miles per hour. The engine, developed from Buick's racing engine, sits exposed at the rear of the car. *Buick Public Relations*

The **1991 Park Avenue Essence** show car was an idealized statement of where Buick's direction in luxury cars would go in the next few years. Its aim was dead-on, as Buicks of the late 1990s followed Essence's lines. *John Heilig*

Design of this Wildcat began in Bill Porter's studio. Dave Rand did the full-size tape drawing that enchanted Porter. "It was the neatest thing I had ever seen," Porter said. "The sketch embodied a successful expression of both muscular sculptural forms—like a crouching cat or a swimming shark—and the exciting mechanical aspects of Buick's latest design technology."

The car was finished in the studio of Kip Wasenko, who designed the Saturns. Ed Roelle headed the development team, with the interior work done by Brian Baker, Nelly Toledo, and Corwin Hanson.

1988 Lucerne

Originally designed as a coupe in 1988, the Lucerne was reworked in 1991 to be a convertible. As a coupe, it was very much related to the contemporary Riviera in that it was a big, elegant four-passenger two-door car. The Lucerne's original design was done by Ted Polack, and executed by Phil Garcia.

The Lucerne was one color, unlike the Riviera Silver Arrow. The bumpers were covered in a body-colored polyurethane skin that made them almost invisible. They seemed molded into the front and rear body forms. In fact, the front end's slope disguised the fact that the leading edge surfaces were bumpers. There was a traditional bumper "shell" on the lower rear end, but the whole was so sleekly filleted into the body form that it went unnoticed. There was a continuity in the surfaces from the base of the windshield to the rear deck. The sides of the Lucerne had a hint of a "Coke bottle" look to them.

The Lucerne was 209.3 inches long on a 113.3-inch wheelbase. The overall length was 22 inches longer than the Riviera's, while the wheelbase was only 6 inches longer, creating longer overhangs. The Lucerne was 72.4 inches wide and 52.2 inches tall, wider and lower than its parent car.

Inside, the Lucerne had an integrated instrument cluster and center console. The interior surfaces were trimmed in burl walnut and leather. All seats were power adjustable. The driver's seat had a memory to retain seat, mirror, and tilt steering wheel positions.

The Lucerne was powered by a 3.8-liter 32-valve V-8 engine, mounted transversely and driving the front wheels.

The power reached the wheels through an electronically controlled four-speed automatic transmission. The Lucerne could be started by touching the key fob, which activated a "Silent Start" system using linear-induction motors.

1989 Park Avenue Essence

While the 1991 Park Avenue was being designed in Bill Porter's production car studio, Phil Garcia was designing the Essence show car in another studio downstairs. The production car ended up with many of the design cues from the dream car.

Originally painted a pale mint green with fish scales in the paint to provide a pearlescent finish, the car was repainted white by Steve Pastiner, who also reworked the wheels and rear end. The windshield wipers were dummies because it wasn't possible to achieve the flushness around the windshield with working wipers at that time.

Porter said, "Essence is the idealized statement of where we hoped Buick's direction in its luxury cars the next few years should stay."

1990 Bolero

Phil Garcia was responsible for the 1990 Bolero, which was smaller than the Essence. The waterfall grille of the Bolero was transferred almost without change to the early 1990s Skylark. "This car has these wonderful little cuddly compact forms," said Bill Porter. "I've always loved the overall compactness of this car: the way that the forms have feeling, as if they're under pressure from the inside, like an egg."

The interior was very organic, according to Porter, and showed human engineering in the fact that all the instruments and all the dials were angled toward the driver and within reach. The gearshift, though, was slanted in the opposite direction.

Under the Bolero's hood was an experimental supercharged 3.3-liter V-6 that produced 206 horsepower. It was mated to an electronically controlled four-speed automatic transaxle that drove the front wheels. The Bolero was 190.1 inches long on a 109.6-inch wheelbase. It was 70.5 inches wide, 53 inches high, and rode on P225/55R16 tires.

1992 Sceptre

This car was initiated to attract new customers to Buick. Then-Buick General Manager Ed Mertz told *Car Design* magazine that Sceptre was a "design statement that could attract these purchasers who have been drawn to international brands."

Bolero was described as an organic car that show human engineering in the fact that all the instruments and dials were angled toward the driver. The waterfall grille of the Bolero was transferred almost without change to the early 1990s Skylark. It was a compact "cuddly" car, according to former chief stylist Bill Porter.
Buick Public Relations

Sceptre was designed with its cabin forward. It had a sharply raked windshield to increase interior space. Inside, the seats were sculptured leather with seating for five. The instrument cluster tilted and telescoped with the steering wheel to ensure driver visibility. Unlike contemporary Buicks, Sceptre was a compact rear-wheel-drive sedan. *Buick Public Relations*

The Sceptre was designed by Jim Bieck, who later went on to design big Chevrolets. The design was cabin forward to increase interior space. Inside, the seats were sculptured leather with seating for five. The instrument cluster tilted and telescoped with the steering wheel to ensure driver visibility.

The Sceptre had its cabin well forward. A sharply raked windshield starts it all, mounted on a wedge-shaped lower body. A short deck completes the package. The front-end graphics are accentuated by the grille and projector headlights.

Unlike contemporary Buicks, the Sceptre was a compact rear-wheel-drive sedan. Under the hood was a super-charged 3.5-liter V-6 that generated 250 horsepower. Buick said it chose rear-wheel-drive because the competitors it was targeting with the car offered rear-wheel drive. And unlike the 1985 Wildcat with its exposed engine, almost none of the engine is visible in the Sceptre. The engine compartment features a "designer cylinder head supercharger cover" and neatly placed fillers for liquids.

1995 XP2000

First shown at the North American International Automobile Show in Detroit in January 1995, the XP2000 was a rear-wheel-drive, four-door sedan that showcased technology designed to make the driving experience more convenient, comfortable, and safe. It had the interior size of a full-size sedan with the exterior dimensions of a midsize sedan. Power came from a 5.0-liter V-8 hooked to a five-speed automatic transmission. Advanced computer controls automatically adjusted the throttle response and other engine characteristics to match different driver desires programmed into the Customer's Choice system. The power-train system would also adjust automatically for different fuels and driving conditions. The XP2000 had computer-controlled air shock absorbers to adjust the ride height and vehicle attitude for improved comfort and maximum aero-dynamic efficiency. The car also had four-wheel anti-lock disc brakes with adaptive vehicle stability and all-speed traction controls.

Among the other features were a passive keyless entry system that could position the car's seats, climate control, and even driving response to a specific driver's tastes; a "Smart Card" setup in which a plastic card could be inserted into the instrument panel, allowing the driver to charge tools, fuel, food, and other services. Also included were a programmable heads-up display (HUD), a navigation system with arrows guiding the driver along a map display, a voice recognition system, automatic guidance and adaptive cruise, near-obstacle detection, and four-position front, side, and rear air bags.

At the heart of the XP2000 was a network of advanced computers that tailored the car to the needs and desires of the individual driver and allowed it to use Intelligent Vehicle Highway Systems planned for the next century. Buick was instrumental in developing cars to ride on these "smart" highways. The XP2000's computers also linked it to the "information superhighway," making it easier for the driver to work and relax in the car.

With P245/45ZR-18 Michelin speed-rated tires at all four corners, the XP2000 put a lot of rubber on the road for a family sedan. The XP2000 was 196.7 inches long on a 115.4-inch wheelbase. It was 73.9 inches wide and 53.5 inches tall, with a curb weight of 3,4000 pounds. The 66-degree windshield angle contributed to the low 0.30 coefficient of drag.

1998 Signia

Introduced at the 1998 North American International Auto Show in Detroit, Signia was a combination sport utility vehicle/station wagon/van/luxury sedan. Buick public relations described it as a "multiple activity vehicle, designed to fully meet the needs of today's active families." The luxury sedan portion of the description was based on the Park Avenue platform used for the Signia.

To ease entry and exit from the Signia, the roof and seats were positioned higher than on traditional automobiles. The seats themselves were angular and finished with deeply pleated leather upholstery. It had wide door openings and inset rocker panels so passengers could get in and sit down without bumping their legs on muddy doorsills. It had cargo space like a station wagon, and the rear maple wood floor would extend 15 inches out the back at the push of a button. The rear hatch was removable for hauling large items, and the rear seats folded to further increase luggage capacity.

XP2000 was a rear-wheel-drive, four-door sedan that showcased technology designed to make the driving experience more convenient, comfortable, and safe. It had the interior size of a fullsize sedan with the exterior dimensions of a midsize. Power came from a 5.0-liter V-8 hooked to a five-speed automatic transmission. *Buick Public Relations*

Signia was a combination sport utility vehicle/station wagon/van/luxury sedan that predicted what the production Rendezvous might look like. Signia was built on a Park Avenue platform. Signia's rear maple wood floor would extend 15 inches out the back at the push of a button. *Buick Public Relations*

The Signia also had infrared warning sensors built in that would detect objects in the vehicle's blind spot and trigger warnings that would be displayed in the outside rearview mirrors.

Painted a brilliant metallic ochre, the Signia made limited use of polished chrome. The moldings were finished in a dark gray-bronze accent tone. The fender sweeps showcased five-spoke chrome-plated aluminum alloy wheels fitted with custom-made Michelin radial tires.

Under the hood was a turbocharged 3.8-liter V-6 pumping out 240 horsepower. The engine drove the front wheels through a four-speed automatic transmission. The Signia also anticipated future powertrain developments. Computer-controlled electric motors could be positioned within each rear wheel hub to automatically deliver torque when wheel-speed sensors signaled the need for enhanced traction.

The Signia also used a reconfigurable "head-down" display monitor. This centrally located color video terminal

Cielo was a four-door midsize family convertible that incorporated advanced technologies, including voice-activated systems to open and close the doors, operate the top, and work entertainment and climate controls. Cielo also used a keyless ignition. *Buick Public Relations*

provided an animated graphic display for controlling five electronic systems: climate control, audio, route navigation, verbal and data communications, and personal computer functions. There was also a reconfigurable "heads-up" display reflected on the windshield.

Built on a 113.8-inch wheelbase platform, the Signia was 185.25 inches long, 74.25 inches wide, and 60.62 inches tall.

1999 Cielo

This four-door midsize family convertible incorporated advanced technologies as its hallmark. These included voice-activated systems to open and close the doors, operate the top, and work entertainment and climate controls. Cielo (Spanish for "sky") also used a keyless ignition. Most gauges and controls were hidden from view until they were needed. They were also reconfigurable, with the driver able to choose fonts, colors, and either analog or digital readings.

Two roof rails strengthened the body and allowed the use of three hard roof panels that slid into the trunk when the driver wanted open-air motoring. The rear window was also adjustable from partially open to fully stored, limiting wind buffeting in the passenger compartment when the top was down. All four doors were power operated and were hinged at the front and rear pillars and opened at the center pillar.

The styling was obviously Buick, with the trademark "waterfall" grille, functional "ventiports," and taillamps running across the entire rear of the vehicle. Power came from Buick's supercharged 3.8-liter V-6 that delivered 240 horsepower. The transmission was an electronic automatic.

Cadillac

Even though Cadillac has been General Motors' nameplate brand from the beginning, when Harley Earl began crafting dream cars, he began with Buick. True, there was the 1933 Aero-Dynamic Coupe, but that car was slated for production and couldn't really be considered a dream car, although it is included here. Bill Mitchell crafted a series of Sixty Specials also in the late 1930s that made his reputation, but these too were production cars, albeit low production.

It wasn't until after World War II that Cadillac finally became the canvas for some works of art. These were customizations of current products, though, and really can't be considered dream cars, although they're also included here.

The first true off-the-wall Cadillac dream car is the 1953 LeMans sports car, which was a Corvette clone with a Cadillac badge. A plethora of dream cars followed, from the 1959 Cyclone to the 1998 Evoq, which is promised for production.

Cadillac may not have been the first General Motors dream car, nor will it be the last, but at the end of the century and millennium, the brand has shown new and exciting activity in the dream car arena, making life more exciting.

1933 V-16 Aero-Dynamic Coupe

Created for the 1933 Chicago "Century of Progress" Exposition, the V-16 Aero-Dynamic Coupe was a streamlined teardrop-shaped fastback coupe with a narrow V-shaped windshield and pontoon fenders. The rear license plate was set into the center of the trunk lid. Built on a 149-inch wheelbase, the coupe was a four-seater with an all-metal roof and aluminum running boards. Gordon Beuhrig, who was working for Cadillac at the time, incorporated the basic shape of this car into the 1936 Cord 810. Cadillac brought the Aero-Dynamic Coupe to production from 1934 through 1937 and built 20 examples. Production versions were also powered by V-8 and V-12 engines on a 146-inch wheelbase. The production V-16-engined cars used a 154-inch wheelbase.

1949 Fleetwood Coupe de Ville

The first Coupe de Ville was introduced at the Transportation Unlimited show more than six months before the production version hit the showrooms. Built on a Sixty Special 133-inch-wheelbase chassis, the Coupe de Ville had a Fleetwood body. Among the special features of the show car were a one-piece curved windshield, simulated scoops on the forward edges of the rear fenders, and chrome scuff plates below the doors. The interior was upholstered in light gray leather. Inside the glove compartment was a short-wave transceiver. GM President Charles E. Wilson, who gave it to his secretary in 1957, later owned this car.

1949 Fleetwood Sixty Special Embassy

One of four show cars built for the 1949 Transportation Unlimited show was the Embassy, a close-coupled limousine built on a Sixty Special chassis. The Embassy had the faux

The V-16 Aero-Dynamic Coupe was created for the 1933 Chicago "Century of Progress" Exposition. Its streamlined teardrop-shaped fastback coupe with narrow V-shaped windshield and pontoon fenders were years ahead of anything on the road at that time. *Cadillac Historical Collection*

El Rancho was another of the 1949 Transportation Unlimited show cars. This was a specially trimmed Series 62 Convertible Coupe with a standard exterior but an interior that had waxed saddle leather upholstery. *Cadillac Historical Collection*

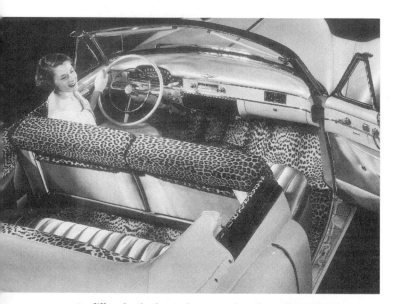

Cadillac built the Debutante for the 1950 Mid-Century Motorama at the Waldorf-Astoria. Debutante was painted Tawny Yellow Buff and was said to have been the inspiration for the play and movie, *The Solid Gold Cadillac*. Cadillac Historical Collection

rear air scoops of the Coupe de Ville as well as a thick horizontal rear fender molding. The Embassy also had a leather-covered roof and a formal rear window. Inside, the front compartment had leather upholstery, while the rear was upholstered in custom-woven broadcloth. The back also had a wide center armrest. There was a glass divider between the compartments with a clock mounted in the header. Accessory equipment included an umbrella, a tool kit with chrome-plated tools recessed in the right front door, and a two-way radio in the front doors.

1949 Series 62 Convertible Coupe El Rancho

Another of the 1949 Transportation Unlimited show cars was El Rancho, a specially trimmed Series 62 convertible coupe. While the exterior was standard, the interior had waxed saddle leather upholstery that was selected from hundreds of hides for color and saddle-stitched in white cord, a leather-covered steering wheel and dash, and gun holsters in the front door pockets. Even the floor was covered in cowhide carpeting. All the interior hardware was silver-plated and engraved.

1949 Fleetwood Sixty Special Caribbean

Finished in a special "Caribbean Daybreak Metallic," this slightly modified Fleetwood Sixty Special was shown at GM's 1949 Transportation Unlimited show at the Waldorf-Astoria Hotel in New York City. Minor exterior changes included leather covering on the sills below the side windows. Inside, the seats were upholstered in French broadcloth and matching leather piping with iridescent green. The instrument panel was painted to match the exterior.

1950 Series 62 Convertible Debutante

For the 1950 Mid-Century Motorama at the Waldorf-Astoria, Cadillac built the Debutante on a Series 62 base. Debutante was painted Tawny Yellow Buff and was said to have been the inspiration for the play and movie *The Solid Gold Cadillac*. The upper interior upholstery was made up of 187 leopard skins from Somaliland. Two pieces of leopard tail were used to make the robe cord, which was attached to the ignition key ring. The lower backs of the seats as well as the cushions were upholstered in gray nylon satin. All the interior hardware was gold-plated, including the keys.

The 1953 Cadillac LeMans was a two-door, two-seat "sports prototype" with a Cadillac flair. LeMans was 400 pounds lighter than a standard Cadillac convertible, thanks to its fiberglass body. The 250 horsepower engine gave "surprising performance," according to *Motor Trend*. *Cadillac Historical Collection*

1952 Golden Anniversary Eldorado

This car was the show-car prototype of the production Eldorado, introduced a year later. It incorporated aircraft-style instruments and dual exhausts that exited through the rear bumper. The wraparound windshield was tinted and heat resistant. Radio antennas were mounted just forward of the rear fins. They would raise and lower automatically. The seatbacks had piping that was in a modern horseshoe pattern with matching door inserts. Door moldings and kick plates were of gold-plated ripple-patterned material.

1952 Townsman

This 50th Anniversary version of the Sixty Special was painted a glistening Nubian black with a golden leather top. Framing the top were moldings of polished stainless steel. Gold metallic emblems were woven into the seat cloth. Townsman also included folding cases for robes, touring equipment, wraps, and other miscellaneous items. These were built into the rear.

1953 LeMans

Unlike the Pontiac of the same name, the 1953 Cadillac LeMans was a two-door, two-seat "sports prototype" with a Cadillac flair. In *Cadillac: The Complete History*, Maurice Hendry calls the LeMans the styling forerunner of the 1954-56 line, and many of the features on the production cars of that era can be seen on the show car.

Several automotive publications of the time had an opportunity to test the LeMans. *Motor Trend* drove it at the GM Proving Grounds and said it had "moderately sensitive steering and good roadholding, but [it was] definitely too heavy and spongy for competition." Still, the LeMans was 400 pounds lighter than a standard Cadillac convertible, thanks to its fiberglass body. The 250-horsepower engine gave "surprising performance," according to *Motor Trend*.

Road & Track called the LeMans "that thing," preferring the El Camino and La Espada dream cars. Motorama visitors had a similar reaction. Crowds surged around the LeMans, but Harley Earl noticed that those who came to the show with money in their pockets showed more interest in the Orleans pillarless four-door sedan.

Cadillac's second, and more popular, 1953 Motorama car was the Orleans, which introduced the four-door hardtop style with no "B" pillar. Orleans also had center-opening doors, with the rear doors hinged at the rear. *Cadillac Historical Collection*

LeMans was built on a 115-inch wheelbase and was 196 inches long. Front-end styling reappeared on 1954 production Cadillacs. It was only 51 inches high at the top of the deeply curved windshield. Power came from a Cadillac V-8 engine rated at 250 horsepower, thanks to a 9.0:1 compression ratio. It was mated to a Hydra-Matic transmission.

LeMans had a memory seat that would automatically move back for entry and egress, then return to the predetermined position when the door was closed. The upholstery was of finest hand-buffed silver-blue leather. The Cadillac crest was embossed on the seat backs. The top was also silver blue and would recess into the rear deck. It had a rain sensor that would automatically raise the top if the car was left out and unattended.

LeMans was redesigned in 1955 with quad headlights and new rear fenders with fins pointier than the originals.

1953 Orleans

Cadillac's second, and more popular, 1953 Motorama car was the Orleans, which introduced the four-door hardtop style with no B-pillar. Cadillac said the absence of the B-pillar offered an extension of airiness for closed cars. Orleans was built on a Series 62 sedan chassis. Besides the absence of the B-pillar, Orleans had center-opening doors, with the rear doors hinged at the rear. Like the LeMans, the Orleans had a wraparound (or panoramic) windshield.

Cadillac's "big" car for the 1954 Motorama was the Park Avenue sedan, built on the 133-inch wheelbase chassis of the Fleetwood Sixty Special. Park Avenue was a fiberglass four-door pillarless hardtop sedan that was 230.1 inches long. *Cadillac Historical Collection*

Orleans was painted Damascus Steel Gray with a contrasting beige vinyl-covered top.

Orleans was also equipped with a standard household electric outlet. A converter produced alternating current and permitted the operation of radios and other electric appliances, such as an electric razor. For the ladies, there was a vanity case. Air conditioning made riding in the Orleans pleasant at any time.

1954 Park Avenue

Cadillac's "big" car for the 1954 Motorama was the Park Avenue sedan, built on the 133-inch-wheelbase chassis of the Fleetwood Sixty Special. The Park Avenue was a fiberglass four-door pillarless hardtop sedan that was 230.1 inches long, more than 19 feet! Under the hood was the standard 230-horsepower V-8. Externally, the Park Avenue introduced the notched roofline, large front-wheel cutouts, and a "reversed" tail fin.

The Park Avenue was painted Antoinette Blue with bright chrome trim. Below the rear deck lid was a special compartment housing the spare tire, covered by a hinged door. The instruments were set in a gray leather-covered panel.

1954 El Camino

Cadillac introduced a pair of two-seaters at 1954 Motoramas. The fiberglass El Camino was built on a 115-inch wheelbase and was 200 inches long, 51.5 inches high, and 79.9 inches wide. It used the standard 230-horsepower V-8. Like many GM dream cars of the era, it had a bubble roof and quad headlights. The tailfin shape appeared again on the 1955 Eldorado convertible. Quad headlights, a fluted side panel, and gull-wing bumpers with bullet tips were all standard Cadillac design elements the following year.

The El Camino incorporated front and rear fiberglass roof saddles that supported the hand-brushed aluminum top. The instrument panel was covered in gray leather, while the insert area behind the instrument dials was hand-brushed aluminum. Below the trunk was a spare tire compartment that was concealed by a hinged door.

1954 La Espada

La Espada was a fiberglass roadster built on a 115-inch wheelbase. It was 200.6 inches long and 51.7 inches high. Among the styling features were metallic trim panels that extended from the front wheel openings to the centers of

El Camino was one of a pair of Cadillacs introduced at 1954 Motoramas. The fiberglass El Camino was built on a 115-inch wheelbase and was 200 inches long, 51.5 inches high, and 79.9 inches wide. Like many GM dream cars of the era, it had a bubble roof and quad headlights. *Cadillac Historical Collection*

La Espada was a fiberglass roadster built on a 115-inch wheelbase. Among the styling features were metallic trim panels that extended from the front wheel openings to the centers of the doors. The wraparound windshield had a 60-degree angle. *Cadillac Historical Collection*

the doors. The wraparound windshield had a 60-degree angle. The La Espada also wore sharp tail fins. Body sheet metal was identical to the El Camino, except La Espada was a roadster and El Camino a coupe.

Painted Apollo gold and trimmed with bright chrome and aluminum, the interior used chrome, aluminum, and high-luster black leather. Behind the seats was a tonneau cover that was later copied by Ford and used in the Thunderbird.

1955 Eldorado Brougham

Cadillac's Eldorado Brougham dream car, introduced at the 1955 GM Motorama, was 7 inches lower and a foot shorter than production Cadillacs. The Eldorado Brougham was a pillarless hardtop with center-opening doors. It had quad headlights and a brushed stainless-steel roof. Among the technical innovations were an air suspension and a swiveling driver's seat that made entry and egress easier.

Built on a 124-inch wheelbase, the Eldorado Brougham was 209.6 inches long, 77.5 inches wide, and 54.4 inches tall. The dash was covered in shock-resistant material that was one of the first padded panels.

1955 LaSalle II

Cadillac built two LaSalle II dream cars for the 1955 Motoramas, resurrecting a nameplate that hadn't been used for 15 years. One of the LaSalles was a small four-door hardtop sedan, powered by a V-6 engine. It wore a slotted vertical grille and concave aluminum panels behind the front wheels that would later be seen on production Corvettes. The second LaSalle II dream car for 1955 was a short two-seat roadster. Similar in design to the four-door hardtop sedan, the roadster had chopped-off front fenders and fully open rear fenders. The exhaust exited through oval pipes in the rocker panels. The LaSalle II sedan used a double-overhead cam V-6 engine. Noteworthy on the sedan was the "dog-leg" A-pillar and compound curve windshield.

1956 Eldorado Brougham Town Car

When the production Eldorado Brougham didn't appear in 1956 as promised, Cadillac kept the flames of desire fanned with two dream cars. The fiberglass-bodied Town Car was built on a 129.5-inch wheelbase and revived open-front town-car styling of the classic era. The rear roof was upholstered in polished black landau leather. The Town Car was 55.5 inches high and 219.9 inches long.

1956 Eldorado Brougham Four-Door Hardtop

Companion to the Town Car was the Eldorado Brougham four-door hardtop. Cadillac historian Walter M. P. McCall called this car a "hyper-luxurious four-door hardtop with a stainless steel roof and every conceivable gadget."

1956 Gala

Cadillac built four other dream cars for 1956 besides the two Eldorado Brougham examples. Gala was also known as "The Wedding Car." It was a richly finished Sedan de Ville four-door hardtop with a pearlescent white and silver finish. The interior upholstery was in ribbed

Cadillac's Eldorado Brougham dream car was seven inches lower and a foot shorter than production Cadillacs. Eldorado Brougham was a pillarless hardtop with center-opening doors. It had quad headlights and a brushed stainless steel roof. Among the technical innovations were an air suspension and a swiveling driver's seat that made entry and egress easier. *Cadillac Historical Collection*

When the production Eldorado Brougham didn't appear in 1956 as promised, Cadillac kept the flames of desire fanned with two dream cars. The fiberglass-bodied Town Car was built on a 129.5-inch wheelbase and revived open-front town car styling of the classic era. *Cadillac Historical Collection*

Gala, also known as "The Wedding Car," was a richly finished Sedan de Ville four-door Hardtop with a pearlescent white and silver finish. Interior upholstery was in ribbed satin, white pearl leather, and mouton fur. *Cadillac Historical Collection*

satin, white pearl leather, and mouton fur. The front doors held small umbrellas with rhinestones on the handles.

1956 Palomino

This dream car was a modified Series 62 convertible coupe. The interior upholstery consisted of natural Palomino hides on the door upper panels, seat backs, and floor mats. The body was painted in beige metallic. Cadillac press releases called it a "ruggedly styled convertible with a shimmering beige metallic body that reflects the Western flair."

1956 Castilian

The Castilian was built on an Eldorado Seville two-door hardtop coupe. Modifications included metallic starlight silver paint and a white textured Vicodec roof. The interior styling was in an "Old Spain" motif with contrasting black and white seat bolsters.

1956 Maharani

The final special 1956 dream car was the Maharani, which was a Fleetwood Sixty Special four-door sedan done in a Far East motif with a rich metallic maroon body and gold-colored roof panel. The Maharani was upholstered in snake skin and satin print with mouton fur carpeting. It had such unusual features as a recessed toaster, folding tables, a hot plate, and a cutlery tray. Cold water was dispensed from tanks installed under the hood. There was also a small safe.

1957 Director

This car was a specially equipped Fleetwood Sixty Special, modified for the busy executive. In this rolling executive suite was a right front seat that would pivot 180 degrees to permit the secretary to take dictation from the executive sitting in the rear seat at a special desk. The Director also carried such necessities as an umbrella, car phone, and turntable.

Palomino was a modified Series 62 Convertible Coupe with interior upholstery that consisted of natural Palomino hides on the door upper panels, seat backs, and floor mats. *Cadillac Historical Collection*

1959 Loewy Cadillac Sedan

Raymond Loewy designed this car for his personal use and had Pichon & Parat in France build it. He retained the center section of the car and redesigned the front and rear. Where the stock Cadillac was rectangular, the Loewy car tapered both front and rear, reducing the width by 14.5 inches. This tapering eliminated the boxy look and gave the big car a more slender, graceful look, according to David H. Ross, writing in *Car Classics*.

Loewy also removed the huge 1959 Cadillac tailfins and grille, which was considered controversial. In place of the grille was a finely perforated screen that was part of the vertical rise of the hood itself that swept from the bumper to the windshield. This screen was augmented by a wide scoop under the front end of the car for air induction at high speed.

Loewy painted the car light gray-blue-green metallic, with a bone-white top.

1959 XP-74 Cyclone

Cadillac was not a company to be outdone by any other, even its fellow GM divisions. So when it came to dream cars, especially in what for Cadillac was the magical year of 1959 and stratospheric fins, GM's luxury division introduced the Cyclone. Like any self-respecting 1959 Cadillac, the Cyclone had two enormous fins. But what were even more dramatic were the two black nose cones that were extensions of the front fenders. These gave the Cyclone a definite rocket-ship appearance.

Cadillac press releases of the time announced some of the Cyclone's features: "A special proximity warning device system is located in the large nose cones that project forward from the front of the fuselage-like fenders. They electronically alert the driver with both an audible signal and a warning light of any automobile or other object he is approaching. The pitch of the signal increases as he draws closer to the object." Sounds like stuff of the 1990s.

Cyclone also had a two-way intercom system that permitted passengers inside the car to talk to people outside the car without having to raise the clear plastic canopy. This canopy was coated with vaporized silver on the inside to deflect the sun's rays. The canopy automatically lifted when either door was opened and could be stored beneath the rear deck. The doors didn't open on hinges: a push button would activate motors that would move the doors out 3 inches. From there they could be slid back to enter the car.

Inside, the Cyclone was replete with aircraft-style instruments. The HVAC system had a knob that would permit the driver to dial in a particular temperature, and the gas heater or air conditioner would automatically maintain that temperature.

Under the hood was a 325-horsepower 390-cubic-inch V-8 engine with a low-profile carburetor, special distributor, cross-flow aluminum radiator, and twin fans. The three-speed automatic transmission was mounted behind the passenger compartment, while the engine's exhaust exited in front of the front wheels. There was also a two-speed rear axle that permitted six forward speeds.

The Cyclone was built on a 104-inch wheelbase, more than two feet shorter than the standard Cadillac of 1959. Its overall length was 196.9 inches. The only obvious feature to make it to production cars were the "skeg" small side fins that also appeared on the Firebird III and later made it to the 1962 Cadillac.

1961 Jacqueline

Pinin Farina had designed a custom Cadillac V-16 boattail speedster in 1931 and had always remained an admirer of Cadillac cars. In 1957 and 1958, the firm built 704 Eldorado Brougham four-door hardtops for Cadillac and wanted to do additional work for the American company. For 1959 and 1960, Farina built four-door six-window hardtop bodies in Turin and fitted them to a 130-inch-wheelbase chassis. But the contract only lasted for 200 examples.

For 1961, still anxious to work with Cadillac, Pinin Farina showed two Brougham dream cars at the Paris *Salon de l'automobile*. Both were hardtops: one a four-door, one a two-door. Both were named Jacqueline in honor of Jacqueline Kennedy, America's First Lady. Since these were

Castilian was built on an Eldorado Seville two-door hardtop coupe chassis. Modifications included metallic starlight silver paint and a white textured Vicodec roof. *Cadillac Historical Collection*

Castilian was built on an Eldorado Seville Two-Door Hardtop Coupe chassis. Modifications included metallic starlight silver paint and a white textured Vicodec roof. *Cadillac Historical Collection*

design concepts, they had no engines. They also had no fins, which was odd for a 1961 Cadillac.

What the Jacqueline designs did have in place of the vertical tailfins were horizontal elements: taillight lenses that wrapped around the fender. Up front was a broad Aston Martin-like grille that stretched from fender to fender. The two-door had a brushed-steel roof and a gold paint scheme. Individual bucket seats were in the front; there were no seats in the rear.

Despite Pinin Farina's efforts, Cadillac wasn't interested. However, in 1987, when Cadillac introduced the Allante, it turned to Pininfarina (as the company was renamed) to build the bodies in Turin and fly them to Hamtramck for installation on the chassis.

1964 Florentine

This car was shown at the 1964 New York World's Fair in the GM Futurama pavilion. Florentine was a custom two-door hardtop. The metal roof had vinyl inserts. The seats were upholstered in embroidered leather. The Florentine returned the full rear wheel opening style and wire wheels to Cadillac design.

1988 Voyagé

Voyagé was a four-passenger test platform that allowed Cadillac engineers to develop and incorporate new features into automobiles that they were designing for the future. Voyagé's aerodynamic profile was outstanding, with a coefficient of drag of just 0.28, making it one of the world's most aerodynamic gasoline-powered vehicles. Part of this efficiency was due to movable front-wheel skirts. The skirts served a dual purpose. During normal driving, they stayed tucked smoothly into the fenders to preserve the clean, aerodynamic lines and allow low drag. When sharp turns were in order, though, the skirts extended out to allow full wheel turns.

The upper surface of the car, from the base of the windshield to the bottom of the taillamps, was a continuous piece of smooth, high-impact tinted glass. Side windows were curved and bent to allow them to serve both an aerodynamic function and add to the styling elements.

The Voyagé was also equipped with high-intensity light-emitting diode (LED) taillamps and turn signals that provided ample warning to approaching vehicles. The lamps were hidden under the glass and formed a continuous strip that was broken in the middle by a rear-vision video camera. The camera's function was to alert the driver to oncoming vehicles by projecting their images on a color monitor located in the instrument panel.

Automatic high-visibility flashers replaced reflectors on the Voyagé. When the vehicle was parked at night and was approached by another vehicle with its headlights on, Voyagé's flashers automatically activated to alert the driver of the oncoming vehicle of another car's presence.

Windshield wipers were completely concealed. When they were needed, the entire wiper mechanism would rise on its own elevator. A cover panel would open briefly to allow the wiper arms to extend into operating position.

Maharani was a Fleetwood Sixty Special four-door sedan done in a Far East motif with a rich metallic maroon body and gold-colored roof panel. It was upholstered in snake skin and satin print with mouton fur carpeting. *Cadillac Historical Collection*

Like any self-respecting 1959 Cadillac, the Cyclone had two enormous fins. But even more dramatic were the two black nose cones extending from the front fenders, which gave the Cyclone a definite rocket ship appearance. Cyclone had a two-way intercom system that permitted passengers inside to talk to people outside the car without having to raise the clear plastic canopy. *Cadillac Historical Collection*

Inside the Voyagé was a hands-off cellular phone, CRT rear vision, navigation, 20-way adjustable seats with memory, and a built-in massager in the seat cushions. The instruments were white-on-black analog. The black background blended in well with the rest of the dash, preserving the car's dignity.

The Voyagé was powered by a 4.5-liter V-8 engine. The port fuel-injected engine developed 275 horsepower and 330 pounds-feet of torque. The increased power enabled sustained 180-miles-per-hour cruising speeds. There was room enough in the engine compartment, though, for the oft-rumored new V-12 that Cadillac was alleged to be developing. The Voyagé was also engineered with a standard all-wheel-drive system and four-wheel disc brakes with electronic anti-lock braking.

The critical dimensions included a 119.6-inch wheelbase, 212.5-inch overall length, 53.4-inch height, and 77.8-inch width.

1998 Evoq

Away from the dream car scene for more than a decade, Cadillac introduced the Evoq in 1998. Evoq was a two-seater with a retractable hardtop that, according to Cadillac, was supposed to show the direction for future Cadillacs. Its charter was strong, as Cadillac announced that the car would enter production before 2005.

Among Evoq's design elements were a strong full-length spline line across the body, a trapezoidal sail, vertical head-lights and taillights, a full-width center high-mounted stop light (CHMSL), and the classic Cadillac egg-crate grille.

Under the hood was a 4.2-liter Northstar V-8 with a fully integrated supercharger/intercooler, four camshafts, continuously variable valve timing, and a new low-friction valvetrain. In this configuration, the engine developed 405 horsepower. In addition, the engine was upgraded with a steel crankshaft, heavy-duty pistons and connecting rods, iron insert main bearing bulkheads, and four-layer head gaskets.

Among the other advanced technologies showcased in the Evoq were Night Vision; the Forewarn backup aid rear obstacle detection system; rear-vision cameras that replace outside rearview mirrors; a vertically anchored tire and wheel system from Michelin; and Communiport, a mobile multimedia information system with voice-activated navigation, e-mail, and entertainment capabilities.

Evoq had pop-up cameras mounted on the doors that were designed to take the place of side- and rearview mirrors. An image was projected on two screens on the center console. Tires were not held to the rims by outward pressure inside the tire, as in conventional vehicles. In the Evoq, the tires were locked to the wheel rim, which radically slowed the rate at which a punctured tire would deflate, allowing the driver to travel as many as 125 miles to get it repaired. Evoq's Night Vision feature, which consisted of an infrared sensor mounted on the front of the car that would give the driver a view of objects well beyond the path of the headlamps, was introduced into production in the 2000 DeVille.

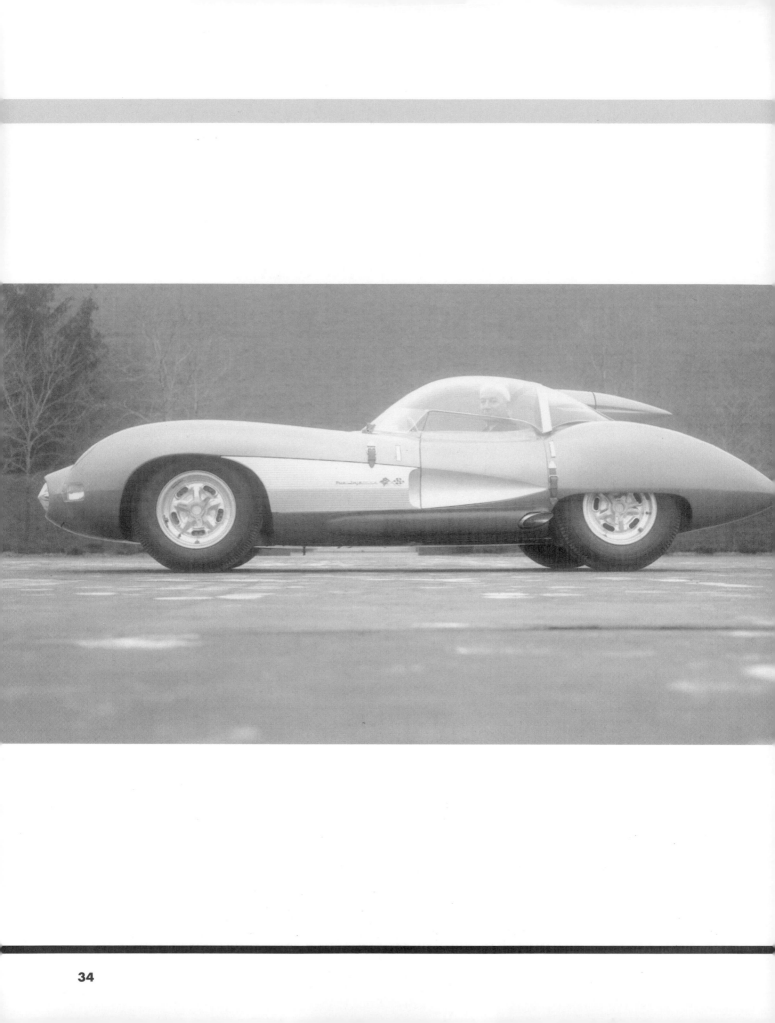

CHAPTER 3

Chevrolet

Chevrolet's first dream car didn't appear on a Motorama stage until 1953, but what a dream car it was. Actually there were three, and all were Corvettes. One made it to production—the convertible. The second made it to production in a totally different form—the Nomad wagon. The third never made it to production—the Corvair fastback—although the name did. In fact, the fastback may have been the most attractive of the three, but who am I to criticize General Motors' designers?

With these three dream cars under their belts, and receiving critical acclaim, Chevy designers took the Corvette theme to every extreme they could. There was the CERV single-seat racer; there were the Bill Mitchell customizations; and there were the experimental versions with the Wankel engine.

Chevy also used the Corvair platform in early years, although as with all manufacturers at the end of the century, the brand is experimenting with an assortment of platforms in its line.

1953 Motorama Corvette

Chevrolet showed three "Corvettes" at the 1953 Motorama. The first was a convertible that was almost identical to the eventual production car except for a downward-facing spear on the side chrome strip, small air scoops in the tops of the fenders, and keyholes in the doors. The Motorama car also had scripted "Corvette" chrome strips above the rear license plate and above the grille. The show car was, in fact, built up from a production car. Corvette was the dream of Ed Cole and Harley Earl. They exhibited the prototype/concept car at the

Detroit Auto Show in 1953. It went into production shortly thereafter with few modifications.

Chevy also showed a fastback version of the Corvette that it called the Corvair. This was a sleek design with a chopped-off rear. It also incorporated hood vents and front fender "gills" for cooling.

The third Corvette was the Nomad station wagon, which was a high-performance two-door wagon. The roofline and rear tailgate design were used on the eventual production Nomads, built from 1955 to 1957.

1955 Biscayne

Chevrolet had begun production of the Corvette and was working on the Corvair. So when the Biscayne was shown in 1955, it is not surprising that it contained design elements of both cars. For starters, the Biscayne's body was built up of "glass fiber reinforced plastic" (fiberglass). Styling from the C-pillar back was obviously Corvair inspired (or would inspire the Corvair), while the side sculpture included a "reverse cove," as compared with the Corvette's.

The front-end styling was unique to the Biscayne, however, although echoes of similar treatment could be seen in other GM cars. The grille consisted of nine vertical chrome pieces that formed part of the front bumper. The "projectile type" front fenders incorporated the parking lights, while

Bill Mitchell had Larry Shinoda design a new body for the chassis of the 1957 SS race car mule. An enclosed-body dragster designed by Tom Tjaarda allegedly inspired the shape. *General Motors Historical Collection*

Chevrolet showed three "Corvettes" at the 1953 Motorama. The first was a convertible that was almost identical to the eventual production car. Chevy also showed a fastback version of the Corvette that it called Corvair. This sleek design had a chopped-off rear. The third Corvette was the Nomad station wagon, which was a high-performance two-door wagon. *General Motors Historical Collection*

The SR-2 Corvette was built with a longer nose and "bullets" over the headlights, fog lamps, an air scoop at the end of the side cove, and a tail fin. A second higher-finned version of the SR-2 was built with the tail fin extending from a head rest behind the driver. *General Motors Historical Collection*

the headlights sat on the hood, giving the Biscayne an Austin-Healey Sprite frog-eye look.

A four-door pillarless sedan, the Biscayne had doors that opened in the center for ease of entry; the front doors were hinged at the front, the rear doors at the rear. The "stratospheric" windshield was not only wraparound, it was wrapover, with a tinted portion that extended into the roof.

While the overall height of the Biscayne was 52.5 inches, good interior headroom was achieved by dropping the floor inside the frame, allowing for lower seats and full head- and legroom. The Biscayne was 10 inches shorter than the standard 1955 Chevrolet. There was a padded instrument panel and dash to protect passengers. All four seats were upholstered in textured white leather. The front seats swiveled outward to ease entry.

Under the hood was an experimental high-compression 215-horsepower V-8 with dual exhausts, a four-barrel carburetor, and a high-lift cam. The transmission was a Powerglide automatic.

1955 L'Universelle

This small van was designed to be nuclear powered, even though no such powerplant existed at the time and probably never will. The styling of the L'Universelle was later reflected in the 1960 rear-engined Corvair van.

1956 SR-2

Harley Earl allegedly had the SR-2 built up because his son Jerry wanted to race a Ferrari. To keep Jerry in the GM family, the SR-2 Corvette was built with a longer nose and "bullets" over the headlights, fog lamps, an air scoop at the end of the side cove, and a tail fin. A second higher-finned version of the SR-2 was built with the tail fin extending from a headrest behind the driver. The SR-2s were used to test high-performance components, such as a heavy-duty suspension system, heavy-duty springs, and a front roll bar.

The dash was engine-turned metal, and the interior door panels were made from concave stainless steel. The doors opened with a rope pull, à la MGA. The trunk was hinged at the bottom. One of the SR-2s was fitted with a bubble top for record runs on Daytona Beach's sands. Buck Baker reached 152.86 miles per hour for the flying mile in the car.

1957 Corvette Super Sport

The SS was designed with twin racing windscreens and a blue racing stripe on a white body. While the front end was stock, the side cove incorporated an SR-2 scoop.

1957 SS

Designed at the behest of Zora Arkus-Duntov, the SS was a purpose-built racer designed in only six months. It had a tapered, sloping tail and a reverse scoop in the side cove that released hot air from the engine compartment. The SS body was built over a chrome-moly tubular space frame that weighed 180 pounds. It used a deDion rear axle and drum brakes that were taken from a Chrysler. Under the hood was a 283-ci iron-block V-8 with aluminum heads, custom headers, and Ramjet fuel injection. It was rated at 307 horsepower. The SS was driven at the Sebring 12 Hours by John Fitch and Pierro Taruffi.

1959 Sting Ray

Bill Mitchell bought the chassis of the 1957 SS race-car mule and had Larry Shinoda design a new body for it. The 1957 Ghia IXG Turin show car allegedly inspired the shape, which was an enclosed-body dragster designed by Tom Tjaarda. The key design features of this car were the sharp-peaked wheel well housings that rose above the body's upper surface. These would appear on the production 1963 Sting Ray. The car was painted silver and had a headrest that sloped back to the tail, like the D Jaguar.

CERV 1 was an open-wheel test bed that was built along Indy car lines with a tubular frame. It was powered by a rear-mounted small-block 283-cubic inch engine that pumped out 350 horsepower. *General Motors Historical Collection*

1959 CERV 1

CERV was an acronym for Chevrolet Engineering Research Vehicle. The car was an open-wheel test bed for Zora Arkus-Duntov that was flexible enough to be able to modify such things as the rear suspension. It also included anti-lock brakes. Built along Indy car lines with a tubular frame, the 1,450-pound car was powered by a rear-mounted small-block 283-cubic-inch engine that pumped out 350 horsepower. Other lightweight parts included a magnesium bell housing and clutch housing.

1960 XP-700

This was a Bill Mitchell-customized Corvette. The side cove contained three scoops to draw air out of the engine compartment. Mitchell had the rocker panels removed and

This Corvair from the initial series was rebodied by Pininfarina primarily to show off the coachbuilder's expertise. The designer gave the Corvair a Porsche-like profile. *General Motors Historical Collection*

Built on 1961 Corvair running gear, the Super Spyder was a two-seater with front-end styling that would indicate the direction Corvair styling was headed. It also had a Jaguar D-Type headrest behind the driver. *General Motors Historical Collection*

installed side exit exhaust pipes in the area. Up front was where the XP-700 varied the most from the stock Corvette. The extended nose contained an oval grille similar to a Ferrari 250GT and even included a prancing horse medallion. For the show circuits, Corvette crossed flags replaced the prancing horse and the opening was made more elliptical. The car was repainted metallic gold for shows, and had a double bubble plexiglass top with a periscope rearview mirror protruding from it. Also added were Dayton wire wheels and Lucas "flame thrower" headlights. Inside, the steering wheel was changed and a metal grid floor was added in the foot well area. Mitchell also had a chronometric stopwatch added as one of the instruments, probably copying a similar installation on a Ferrari Superamerica by Pininfarina.

1960 Pininfarina Corvair

This Corvair from the initial series was rebodied by Pininfarina primarily to show off the coachbuilder's expertise. The Italian designer chose to give the Corvair a Porsche-like profile and showed the car at European auto shows in 1960 and 1961.

1961 XP-755 Shark

This Bill Mitchell concept car was designed by Larry Shinoda. The Harley Earl influence remained with the dou-

ble bubble roof of the XP-700. On the rear deck lid were pop-up doors that were part of an emergency brake system. This car was first displayed at Elkhart Lake, Wisconsin, in the summer of 1961. It was a direct descendant of the racing Sting Ray. Mitchell used a fish he had caught off Bimini as the inspiration for the car's color scheme, which featured a white underbody that blended into a dark iridescent blue upper body. Like some earlier show cars, the Shark had flush door handles that popped out when a button was pushed.

The original Shark had vents for the supercharger hump in the center of the hood with the words "SUPERCHARGER" alongside them. Later, when the car was redesigned and renamed "Mako Shark," the vents disappeared. Thermostatically controlled vents automatically opened to release excess heat instead. According to Mark Jordan, son of GM Design Vice President Chuck Jordan, the Shark was built on the XP-700 frame. It copied the metal gridwork foot wells of the previous car. Also added was a wood-rimmed steering wheel with a Ferrari prancing horse in the center, a gift to Mitchell from Enzo Ferrari.

The Shark was powered by a 325-cubic-inch V-8 with four side-draft carburetors and a supercharger nestled in the engine's vee. It was rated at 456 brake horsepower.

1962 Corvair Sebring Spyder

Built on a 93-inch wheelbase, the Sebring Spyder was a two-seater with a pointed nose and a sculpted body. Only the doors were unmodified on this car. This was a Bill Mitchell idea car that used a Paxton supercharger and had extensive suspension changes to accommodate the added power.

1962 Corvair Super Spyder

Built on 1961 Corvair running gear, the Super Spyder was a two-seater with front-end styling that would indicate the direction Corvair styling was headed. It also had a Jaguar D-Type headrest behind the driver. Power came from a turbocharged version of the Corvair air-cooled six-cylinder engine that was rated at 150 horsepower. Behind the rear wheel wells were three exhaust pipes. The Super Spyder was 173.3 inches long on a 93-inch wheelbase. The body

The Corvair Monza GT Coupe used a modified Corvair engine that was placed ahead of the rear axle rather than behind it as in the stock car. The fiberglass-bodied Monza Coupe featured four-wheel independent suspension and four-wheel disc brakes. *General Motors Historical Collection*

was shortened from the stock Corvair by cutting out 15 inches between the doors and rear wheels.

1962 Corvair Monza GT Coupe

Built for the 1962 New York International Automobile Show, the Monza GT used a modified Corvair engine that was placed ahead of the rear axle, rather than behind it as in the stock car. The fiberglass-bodied Monza Coupe featured four-wheel independent suspension and four-wheel disc brakes. While louvers covered the rear windows, the entire rear end of the passenger compartment of the car hinged forward to ease entry and exit as well as provide access to the engine. The seats were fixed and the pedals were adjustable as in the Ford Mustang I.

The Monza GT was built on a 92-inch wheelbase, had a 53-inch track, and was 42 inches tall. Chevrolet also built a convertible version—the Monza SS—with a windshield that encircled the driver and had a conventional Corvair engine location.

Former GM Director of Design David Holls called the Monza GT "one of the best cars we ever made. It was a significant car in that others followed it. It was very dramatic. It drove very well. It was a little feather of a car—very lightweight. It drove beautifully and handled beautifully. I would have loved to have gone into production with that car. It was a sweetheart; such a refined little car."

1963 Corvette Rondine

This show car was built by Pininfarina on a 1963 Sting Ray chassis. It incorporated two roofline designs, a reverse-slope rear window, and a more conventional sloping rear window. The rear fender lines resembled those of the Fiat 124 because American expatriate Tom Tjaarda designed both cars.

1963 Corvair Testudo

Designed by Bertone and shown at the 1963 Geneva Salon, the Corvair Testudo had sleek, rounded lines, a forward-hinged roof and windshield, and ultra-reclining seats.

1964 CERV 2

The CERV 2 was the second of Zora Arkus-Duntov's racing test beds. Larry Shinoda and Tony Lapine designed

Bertone designed the Corvair Testudo and showed it at the 1963 Geneva Salon. The car had sleek, rounded lines, a forward-hinged roof and windshield and ultra-reclining seats. *General Motors Historical Collection*

this four-wheel-drive midengined sports car. Two torque converters were installed, front and rear. This was the first midengined car to have permanent four-wheel drive.

1964 Corvette XP-819

Larry Shinoda designed the XP-819. It had a front hood vent that allowed warm air from the radiator to exit the car. It had a tapered nose, a design feature that would be carried forward on the Corvair Monza.

Chevy shipped the rear-engined XP-819 to Daytona speed merchant Smokey Yunick to be dismantled. Yunick accomplished half the job by cutting the frame in half and putting all the parts in an unused paint booth. But the car was later rescued when Yunick held a "garage sale" and reassembled it.

1965 Corvette Mako Shark II

While Mako Shark I was a version of the original Shark, Mako Shark II was its own vehicle. It had a removable roof to offer better access to the seats, which led to removable roof hatches in 1968-82 production Corvettes. The paint scheme was dark on the top and light on the bottom, like a shark Mitchell had caught while fishing. The car

Astro I was a fiberglass Corvair-based fastback coupe that had a two-piece body. Like the Monza GT before it, the entire rear section lifted, although in this case the seats lifted as well. *General Motors Historical Collection*

also made extensive use of flat black paint rather than chrome. Under the hood was a 427-cubic-inch V-8 at one time; later Mitchell installed an aluminum-block ZL-1. The headlight covers slid back into the body to reveal French-made lenses. The rear roofline featured louvers over the glass, which could turn flat with a button. Even the rear bumper would extend at the push of a button. The Mako Shark II used rectangular exhaust pipes on the clay model, but had six round pipes on the running car. On the clay, Mitchell installed an aircraft-style wheel, numerous gauges, and the metal gridwork floor of the XP-700. The running version had a more conventional steering wheel and a digital dash.

When the Mako Shark was shown again at the 1966 New York International Automobile show, the under-the-door outside exhaust headers were gone and the side of the body had been cleaned up, making it appear closer to a production car.

The Mako Shark II reappeared in 1969 as the Manta Ray, with the addition of a front spoiler and some grille protection. Engine exhaust exited through side pipes again. The legend "ZL-1" was now on the hood bulge. A flat rear deck

replaced the rear window louvers. Instead of the Mako Shark II's bobbed tail, the Manta Ray had a long tapering tail. When the driver applied the brakes, two panels would lift on the rear deck to reflect brake lights to following cars.

1967 Astro I

This fiberglass-bodied Corvair-based fastback coupe had a two-piece body. Like the Monza GT before it, the entire rear section lifted, although in this case the seats lifted as well. The engine was a single-overhead cam, 167-cubic-inch, 200-horsepower flat six with hemispherical combustion chambers.

1968 Astro-Vette

A pure dream car with no headlights, the low Astro-Vette had an airfoil behind the rear seat and full rear fender skirts over the rear wheels. These skirts were hinged at the top if access to the rear wheels was necessary. Behind the front wheels were four cutlines to simulate flaps that could be opened to release heat from the engine compartment.

XP-882 was introduced at the 1970 New York Auto Show. The mid-engined Corvette housed a 455-cubic inch Corvette V-8 engine mounted transversely between the rear wheels. For a transmission, the XP-882 used a version of the GM Hydra-Matic used on the Oldsmobile Toronado and Cadillac Eldorado. *General Motors Historical Collection*

AeroVette, designed for a four-rotor Wankel engine, had a gull-wing design. When the car finally appeared, the rotary engine program had been scrubbed and the engine replaced by a V-8. The design featured a long tapering nose and tail that were constructed of soft material. *General Motors Historical Collection*

1968 Astro II

A midengined derivative of the XP-880, which in itself was an update of XP-819, the Astro II still required wider rear wheels and tires. The entire rear section lifted to expose the engine. This car also had no provision for headlights.

1969 Mulsanne

Bill Mitchell customized a street car into the 1969 AeroCoupe. It incorporated new side pipe designs as well as different spoilers. The roof hatch was hinged at the rear and swung up to make entry and exit easier.

In 1970, the AeroCoupe was reworked as the Mulsanne, named after the main straightaway at Le Mans. In this form it was customized even further. The Mulsanne had fixed headlights behind clear covers. In the hood were two functional scoops that fed air to the ZL-1 engine. The outside rearview mirrors were also mounted higher than on production cars.

1970 XP-882

This Corvette was introduced at the 1970 New York Auto Show and was so convincingly done that *Road & Track* announced in January 1971 that this *was* the 1973 Corvette. Sadly, it was not to be. The midengined Corvette housed a 455-cubic-inch Corvette V-8 engine mounted transversely between the rear wheels. For a transmission, the XP-882 used a version of the GM Hydra-Matic used on the Oldsmobile Toronado and Cadillac Eldorado, except turned around since those two cars were front-wheel drive. A silent chain transferred power from the torque converter to the gearbox.

The frame was welded steel with some tubes in the design that would have taken Corvette away from the rigid-ladder frame that it had been using. The outer panels were to be fiberglass with the basic steel structure performing all the structural work. In the hood were two circular panels that could be lifted to refill fluids.

The XP-882 was built on a 95.5-inch wheelbase, slightly shorter than the stock Corvette's. The show car also had an external trunk opening, something that had been absent from Corvette for many years and did not reappear until the 1990s. The spare tire was mounted in the front behind the radiator. The dramatic fastback styling included louvers at the sides of and over the rear window and a "boattail" effect with the rear window tapering down to the rear bumper.

"Electric window lifts will be standard," *R&T* wrote. "Air conditioning will be at least optional, maybe standard; and we can expect it to be really adequate, well designed air conditioning with fresh-air intake as on American sedans."

The styling of the XP-882 influenced Corvettes of the 1980s and early 1990s, without the louvered rear window and, of course, without the midengine location.

1973 XP-897

This Corvette was a test bed for the GM version of the two-rotor Wankel rotary engine. Pininfarina built the body and used smaller wheels than were on the original clay model. This was a full fastback with the hatch covering the engine and trunk. There was an air-extraction vent over the rear window that allowed engine heat to exit. The two-rotor engine was transversely mounted ahead of the luggage compartment.

The Corvette Indy concept car received its name because in the engine compartment rested the twin turbo Chevrolet Indy engine. The Corvette Indy had all-wheel drive, all-wheel steering, anti-lock brakes, traction control, and an active suspension assembly. *General Motors Historical Collectio*

Venture was a sports sedan that was trumpeted as a complete GM car. Venture's passengers sat in individual bucket seats, two in front and two in the rear. The front passengers were wrapped in a continuous surface that flowed from the sides of the center console to the doors. *General Motors Historical Collection*

1977 AeroVette

Designed to accept a four-rotor Wankel rotary engine, the AeroVette had a gull-wing design. When the car finally appeared, the rotary engine program had been scrubbed and the engine replaced by a V-8. Chuck Jordan supervised the design of the car, which featured a long tapering nose and tail that were constructed of soft material. This car is unique in that the A-pillar is concealed behind the wraparound windshield. The bifold doors didn't extend beyond the width of the body. When fully lifted and combined with a low door sill, entry and exit were relatively easy.

1984 Ramarro

This lime-green Corvette dream car was built by Bertone. It incorporated sliding doors and a nose that was more aerodynamic than the standard production car. The radiator and air-conditioning condenser were relocated to the rear of the car. Seating was unique and consisted of a leather "saddle" draped across the center console.

1986 Corvette Indy

The Corvette Indy concept car was first shown to the public at the Detroit Auto Show in January 1986. Chevrolet Chief Engineer Don Runkle said at the introduction, "We do these cars as much for inspiration as excitement, because it gives our people a chance to turn their dreams into reality." This version of the Corvette received its name because in the engine compartment rested the twin turbo Chevrolet Indy engine. The Corvette Indy had all-wheel drive, all-wheel steering, anti-lock brakes, traction control, and an active suspension. Power was delivered to all four wheels through a torque-split box with three differentials. Inside, a TV screen provided rearward vision thanks to a camera mounted in the back. Two other screens mounted on the doors gave information on vehicle dynamics, navigation, and engine operation. The doors also held individual climate and sound system controls. The computer-controlled wheel control system employed a sensor to read the accelerator pedal position

and feedback to the accelerator by means of an electric motor. The system electronically limited wheelspin. Also, the ABS sensors sent information to the wheel control computer when the car was accelerating. Wheel and suspension response was optimized electronically for all conditions, making it possible to maintain ride quality without compromising handling. Input from the wheel control system computer altered suspension compliance instantly to absorb bumps or to stiffen it for cornering.

When the car was shown in 1988, a four-cam, 32-valve 350-cubic-inch V-8 that developed 380 horsepower had replaced the Indy engine. The engine was designated 350/32. This engine was engineered specifically for transverse applications, according to Chevrolet, with four valves per cylinder for efficient combustion chamber airflow. It had alloy cylinder heads with two chain-driven camshafts per bank and narrow-edge pent-roof combustion chambers. The engine was capable of developing 380 horsepower at 6,000 rpm and 370 foot-pounds of torque at 3,800 rpm.

The Corvette Indy was built off a carbon-fiber torque tube backbone. This filament-wound beam connected the front suspension to the engine/rear suspension assembly. High modulus carbon fibers were wound at optimum angles for different modes of stiffness. The body platform was attached to this backbone structure. Chevy chose a carbon fiber/Nomex composite construction to achieve high strength with ultra-low mass. The use of composites provided a weight advantage of approximately 2.4:1 over conventional steel.

The Corvette Indy was also designed to incorporate four-wheel steering. The rear-wheel steering system would augment conventional front-wheel steering.

By 1988, the exaggerated lines of the original car were softened and a T-bar roof was added for structural rigidity.

The Corvette Indy was 189.0 inches long on a 98.2-inch wheelbase. It was 42.9 inches tall. Estimated top speed was in excess of 180 miles per hour, with a 0-60 miles-per-hour time of less than 5.0 seconds and a 0-100 miles-per-hour time of less than 10.9 seconds.

1987 Express

Introduced at the 1987 Detroit Auto Show, the Express was described as a concept car for high-speed intercity travel. Designed at GM's Advanced Concept Center in California, the Express showed dramatic aerodynamics, with one single surface from the front bumper back to the taillights. Its drag coefficient was a phenomenal 0.195. Designers were asked to develop a four-seat car that had a top speed of 150 miles per hour. The Express was driven by a gas turbine engine, chosen because of its low-speed torque. Called AGT-5, the turbine was fitted with a system that retrieved exhaust gas heat and used it to warm intake air. The engine was mounted ahead of the rear axle to eliminate having the hot exhaust pipes pass under the passenger compartment. The Express was built with a steel frame and a reinforced resin body. Inside there were five CRT displays: three for rearview vision, one for instruments, and one for a navigation system.

1988 Venture

Unlike the minivan that would appropriate the name in the late 1990s, the 1988 Venture was a sports sedan that was trumpeted as a complete GM car. In fact, it was advertised as a GM-UAW car, to reflect the contributions of the autoworkers' union in its development. It was the hourly work force that chose the name Venture.

The Venture's passengers sat in individual bucket seats, two in front and two in the rear. Instrumentation and controls had a definite sporty theme. The two front passengers were wrapped in a continuous surface that flowed from the sides of the center console to the doors. The console continued back through the rear seats. The front seats were power adjustable in 15 directions. The side and lower bolsters would fold away when the doors were opened to facilitate entry and exit.

Under the Corvette-like hood was a 3.1-liter V-6 with aluminum cylinder heads and multiport fuel injection. The engine would later make it to production.

The Venture rode on a long wheelbase and had sharply sloped front and rear windshields. Its sportiness was gained from its lower visual center of gravity, as well as the 17-inch Goodyear tires. In the boundary line between the greenhouse and the lower body was a definite "kink" that served to set it apart from most production cars.

1988 CERV III

Developed concurrently with the Corvette Indy, the CERV III was a product of GM Corporate Engineering with input from Lotus. The goal of the CERV III was to translate the Corvette Indy to a street car. The nose was shortened and the severely curved side windows were modified to permit normal roll-up windows. The engine was a 650-horsepower ZR-1/LT-5 engine that used two Garrett turbochargers.

Developed concurrently with the Corvette Indy, the CERV III was a product of GM Corporate Engineering with input from Lotus. The nose was shortened and the severely curved side windows were modified to permit normal roll-up windows. *General Motors Historical Collection*

1990 Nivola

Designed and built by Bertone, the Nivola used a hydropneumatic suspension, similar to that used in the MG1100 sedan. The suspension would adjust to variations in load and road surface. The engine was a ZR-1/LT-5 V-8 mated to a ZF five-speed manual gearbox. The midlocated engine compartment would also house the hard top when it was lowered. Luggage was stored in the doors, which were a foot wide.

1999 Nomad

Like its namesake of more than 40 years earlier, the Nomad sport wagon combined the performance and handling of a sport sedan with the access and flexibility of a sport utility vehicle. The Nomad was intended to be a driver's car, and was equipped with a small-block Chevrolet V-8 engine, independent rear suspension, and shift-by-wire transmission.

The Nomad styling features included venetian-blind-type slots that kicked up and slid forward, exposing a 36-inch opening in the roof. The rear seats folded flat, and the front seat folded forward to allow additional storage for long cargo. The rear tailgate folded down and slid away to allow easier access and loading.

1999 Triax

Based on the small Tracker sport utility, Triax was designed at the Center for Creative Studies in Detroit. The name comes from the tread pattern in the tires, which is a repeated landscape that leaves scenic impressions in the dirt during off-road excursions. The same pattern was used on the seats and instrument panel.

The interior trim was made from outdoor sport materials such as bungee cord and netting. There was even a state-of-the-art backpack included.

Chrysler

In the 1950s, Chrysler dream cars were usually designed by Virgil Exner and were often built by Ghia in Italy. Exner had an uncanny eye for the dramatic. His "Forward Look" cars of the era set styling trends that sent other designers and manufacturers scrambling to imitate. It could be said that Exner's use of tail fins, while coming later than those of Harley Earl at GM, may have inspired Earl's excesses in the 1959 Cadillac and other GM cars.

Today, the Chrysler Corporation dream cars are penned under the supervision of Tom Gale and John Herlitz. Gale may rightly be considered one of the architects of Chrysler's rebirth. His minivan designs were just the right combination of practicality and sportiness to attract the greater majority of buyers. With greater corporate responsibility, Gale has ceded some of the design responsibility to John Herlitz, who has shown that he's no slouch when it comes to overseeing the creation of exciting automobiles. Under Herlitz, Chrysler Corporation's dream cars (including those of Plymouth, Dodge, and Jeep) have shown drama in design and innovation in powerplants. Once again it is Chrysler that gives life to automotive enthusiasts' fantasies.

1941 Newport

Introduced at the same time as the Thunderbolt, the Newport had classic fender sweeps that predated the side sculpturing of the MGA in a dual-cowl phaeton format. The body enveloped the rear wheels with full fender skirts, while the front grille and pop-up headlamps resembled the Cord 810. The Newport was based on a design by Ralph Roberts, who was manger of LeBaron, and was designed by Alex Tremulis. This car was used to pace the 1941 Indianapolis 500 race and was the first nonproduction car to earn such honors.

Tremulis and Roberts, working for Briggs, LeBaron's bodybuilders, presented a series of sketches to K. T. Keller, then president of Chrysler, that were based on a group of Land Speed Record cars. Alongside each of these cars was a sketch of a streamlined passenger car. Tremulis suggested that they be built without nameplates, but their heritage was obvious because of Chrysler's philosophy that "function dictates form and that beauty is the by-product of sheer engineering integrity." Chrysler was still reeling from the Airflow flops, however, and was nervous about streamlining, but these concepts presented by Tremulis and Roberts hit a note.

Keller endorsed the Newport and Thunderbolt as parts of a traveling road show, much like GM's similar events. But Keller's idea was to have six shows running simultaneously, so six cars had to be built rather than just one. Chrysler ads of the time said, "Take a good look at the Newport's basic design. A few years from now you will find that it has had a profound influence on the future." They were correct. Within a few years (and after a few more for World War II), cars had full-width bodies with faired-in fenders and no running boards. The front and rear fenders were blended together and the hood had a lower profile.

The 1941 Newport had classic fender sweeps that predated the side sculpturing of the MGA in a dual-cowl phaeton format. The body enveloped the rear wheels with full fender skirts. It was used to pace the 1941 Indianapolis 500 race, and was the first nonproduction car to earn such honors. *Daimler Chrysler Historical Collection*

Designed at the same time as the Newport, the Thunderbolt was a huge two-seater with a retractable steel roof. The car featured fully enclosed wheels and a ribbed rocker panel that accentuated its aerodynamic shape. *Daimler Chrysler Historical Collection*

The Newport's phaeton body was hand-formed from aluminum sheet. The headlights were recessed and covered. Under the headlight panels were streamlined, detailed parking lights. Instead of door handles, the Newport used push buttons. The tonneau that covered half of the rear passenger space could be raised hydraulically at the touch of a button to swallow the top. The flowing front fenders that sloped gradually to the rear then swept up and over the rear wheels were amazingly like what would appear after World War II on the Jaguar XK120 and MGA.

The top itself was made from English-made Burbank cloth and was braced with all-metal bows. Side curtains replaced side windows.

Built on the 1941 Crown Imperial chassis, the Newport had a 145.5-inch wheelbase. Power came from a 323.5-cubic-inch straight-eight engine that used nine main bearings.

The K-310 was an "idea car" designed by Virgil Exner and built at Ghia's Turin studio. It influenced Chrysler Corporation's "Forward Look" cars of the 1950s. For example, the K-310's "microphone taillights" that rose above the rear fender were adopted for the 1955-56 Imperial. *Daimler Chrysler Historical Collection*

The Chrysler C-200 was based on the New Yorker and was essentially a convertible version of the K-310. Chrysler advertised the C-200 as "a prototype of the dramatic new convertible." *Daimler Chrysler Historical Collection*

Roberts said, "The Newports were lovely things to ride in. They moved with the swift, solid stately comfort of a Pullman car. Of course they weren't sports cars in any sense involving competition. But performance wasn't a consideration on that project. The Newport was designed to be used as a basis for prediction—and as a beautiful thing to look at and enjoy."

1941 Thunderbolt

A huge two-seater, the Thunderbolt had a retractable steel roof. It was designed by Roberts, although Tremulis also had a hand in penning it. The name was taken from the Land Speed Record car driven by Capt. George E. T. Eyston. Tremulis called the Thunderbolt, "The first streamlined car without individual fenders." The car featured fully enclosed wheels. A ribbed rocker panel accentuated the Thunderbolt's aerodynamic shape. The Thunderbolt featured an electrically operated retractable hardtop that withdrew into the trunk. Like the Y-Job that preceded it, the Thunderbolt had concealed headlamps, power windows, and doors that opened with the push of a button. LeBaron's custom body shop at Briggs built six examples of the Thunderbolt in 1940 on a C-26 chassis that had a 127.5-inch wheelbase. Inside, the front seat was a red-leather-covered bench.

Roberts' first version of the Thunderbolt had a reverse-sloped windshield, with the top more forward than the bottom. According to Tremulis (in *SIA*, Number 28), "Ralph had flown in a rainstorm with a pilot whose plane had a strange windshield that swept out at the top instead of the bottom. This pilot claimed that rain water flew right off, and that this curious design eliminated wind noise, too." They tried the design on the Thunderbolt, but the Chrysler people wouldn't buy it.

Unlike the Newport, the Thunderbolt had a symmetrical dash, with glove boxes on both sides. The instrumentation was simple and centrally mounted, with a large speedometer and clock, and smaller accessory gauges. The radio was centrally mounted. The left-side glove box contained all the switches necessary to operate the top and rear deck.

With its aerodynamic "bathtub" styling, it was sometimes difficult to tell if the Thunderbolt was coming or going.

The Special was the third car in the marriage between Chrysler and Ghia. This two-passenger sports sedan was built on a 125.5-inch-wheelbase New Yorker chassis. It had a fold-down rear bench jump seat that could be used for additional seating. *Daimler Chrysler Historical Collection*

The 1953 Special Modified used the same sheetmetal forms as the Special but it was built on the 125.5-inch-wheelbase New Yorker chassis. Still, it was 10 inches shorter than the Special. Two copies of this car were built, incorporating the K-310 styling features of open wheel wells, sculptured fenders, short rear deck, and long front deck. *Daimler Chrysler Historical Collection*

It had a large rear deck, matching the front hood that left room for a lot of luggage, even when the top was retracted.

1952 K-310

An "idea car" designed by Virgil Exner and built at Ghia's Turin studio, the K-310 had an influence on the Chrysler Corporation "Forward Look" cars of the 1950s. For example, the K-310 had "microphone taillights" that rose above the rear fender; Chrysler adopted them for the 1955-56 Imperial. *Road and Track* (in 1952 the ampersand hadn't entered the masthead) didn't like the taillights. The reviewer wrote, "Whoever came up with the microphone-type tail lights will probably get an offer from National Broadcasting Company, but this type of 'last minute' effort nearly ruins a clean design."

The K-310 had an eagle on the grille; the Imperial had an eagle between its twin grilles. One feature that didn't make it to production was the "blister" front fenders of the K-310. They were too difficult to implement in a production car at the time. The K-310 had open wheel arches that exposed the rubber. Most dream cars of the era went the other way, with fender skirts on the rear wheels and front wheels as well. The original plan was to use knock-off hubs on the 17-inch Borrani wire wheels, but they weren't available for the display model and the wheels were bolted on.

The K-310 used the new cast-iron Chrysler Fire Power 331-cubic-inch V-8 engine, combined with Hydra-Guide power steering. It combined four carburetors, larger valves, an 8:1 compression ratio, and modified valve timing to increase output by 25 horsepower to 310.

Built on the 125.5-inch-wheelbase Saratoga chassis, the K-310 was 59 inches tall. The finish was two-tone blue and included a wraparound rear window. Inside, the upholstery was blue and gray leather. The front seats slid forward when the backs were tilted to provide easier access to the rear seats. There were bench seats front and rear, making the K-310 a six-seater. A unique feature from sports car practice was the steering wheel with drilled-out spokes.

In a paper he presented to the Detroit Chapter of the Society of Automotive Engineers, Virgil Exner wrote the following, which explains some of the design theories of the time:

This car was designed here in Detroit in a special studio entirely separated from our regular styling programs. To insure secrecy, we had considered building this car abroad. Our minds were definitely made up when the Korean war filled our shops and occupied the full time of our own excellent craftsmen. We selected Ghia, of Turin, Italy . . . because

D'Elegance used a horizontal line starting at the front fender and arching up over the rear wheel as a style feature. It also had a sloping rear window and "donut deck" that included a spare tire impression that actually covered the spare tire. *Daimler Chrysler Historical Collection*

Le Comte, the "male" New Yorker Deluxe Sedan, was painted bronze with a black roof. It too had a color-coordinated interior, wire wheels, and a continental spare tire kit. *Daimler Chrysler Historical Collection*

he is one of Europe's greatest designers, one of the best body builders in the world and . . . an old friend of ours. We knew he could execute beautifully the new design we had created in Detroit.

The premise on which this car was designed was simply that an automobile cannot be properly styled unless it is first conceived as a whole unit. It must be created as a unity—from bumper to bumper. The theme must be a single one to which all components are intimately related. Concentration on various parts such as fenders, top, front end, etc., is not possible until the over-all picture is clearly established. The ornamentation must be used to accentuate existing highlights, not to create new ones.

To achieve this unity it is necessary to integrate carefully each and every detail into one harmonious theme. The headlight placement was designed to give the car character and to set it apart from "flush-sided" cars.

The wheel, one of man's oldest and most vital inventions, is one of the purest and most beautiful designs. It is, likewise, the essence of functional automotive design. Why attempt to hide it? Historically, large-diameter wire wheels have been associated with sports and racing cars of top caliber. The large diameter wheel also gives a better proportion to the over-all style of the car, further helping to create an impression of lowness. In addition to these historical and design considerations, the large diameter wire wheels allow better brake cooling and extend the tire life. It is for these reasons that we chose these wheels as the keynote of the car styling and emphasized their function by the fender treatment.

The original design included a spare tire that was mounted in the deck lid. Later we decided to leave the imprint on the deck lid and recess the tire in the trunk floor. This gave us the opportunity to check the public reaction to both designs.

The instrument panel, often referred to as the fashion mark of the interior, was styled to accentuate the simplicity and functional design which sports and racing cars have

made famous. The large, round, legible instruments were functionally designed to look like instruments and were carefully placed for the driver's convenience.

The front end provided a familiar and difficult problem—that of identifying the car without recourse to excessive decorative treatment. First, we determined the smallest round opening that would allow satisfactory cooling performance. Then we designed a modern modification of the traditional radiator shape. The engraved coat of arms on the grille was chosen to symbolize the character of this model in conjunction with the lamps and bumper so that the whole would present a simple, integrated theme.

In brief, we feel that the K-310 is entirely an American design, incorporating line, surface, and highlight themes that integrate the design into a simple unity. It is traditional in that the lines are strong and classic. It is functional and modern in

One of Virgil Exner's "idea cars," the Falcon was built by Ghia, who helped bring many of Exner's creations to metal. This was a two-passenger roadster built on a 105-inch-wheelbase chassis. Exner noted that the Falcon took its inspiration from jet fighters and boats, which have pronounced wedge shapes. *Daimler Chrysler Historical Collection*

Another of Exner's "idea cars," the Flight Sweep I featured dramatic wedge-shaped styling. The rear fenders were swept up into a fin, as with Exner's "Forward Look" production cars. *Daimler Chrysler Historical Collection*

that we emphasize the wheels and feeling of an automobile. It represents simplicity in that the whole design, bumper to bumper, is perceptually unified.

1952 C-200 Cabriolet

The Chrysler C-200 was based on the New Yorker. The C-200 was essentially a convertible version of the K-310, although the K-310 was based on the Windsor. The styles of the two cars were basically identical. Chrysler advertised the C-200 as "a prototype of the dramatic new convertible."

The C-200 used a basically stock FirePower Hemi V-8 engine that drove through a Fluid Torque automatic transmission. "Its sports car roadability," read Chrysler advertising, "is enhanced by the Chrysler Corporation Power Steering that is already recognized as an extraordinary innovation for full-time control and driving ease."

A Chrysler brochure of the time stated, "Standing a rakish five feet from pavement to top of windshield, the C-200 with its distinctive accoutrement and new elan of

The 1960 Dart was designed by Virgil Exner with a sloping nose and "bat wing" tailfins that were deemed too radical for their time. *Daimler Chrysler Historical Collection*

line and manner captures the jaunty air of the sports car, subtly interpreting the bold motif suggested in its fully exposed wire wheels."

Instrumentation consisted of a large tachometer and speedometer flanking the steering wheel, with small circular dials indicating fuel supply, oil pressure, engine temperature, and amperes extending across the panel to the right.

Built on a 125.5-inch wheelbase, the C-200 wore 17-inch chrome-plated wire wheels. It had self-energizing disc brakes and those magnificent "microphone taillights."

1952 Chrysler Special

This was the third car in the marriage between Chrysler and Ghia. A departure from the K-310 and C-200, the Special, a two-passenger sports sedan, was built on a 125.5-inch-wheelbase New Yorker chassis. It also had a fold-down rear bench jump seat that could be used for additional seating, but like the Mercedes-Benz 300SL, it was used primarily for the matched set of luggage that came with the car. The Special was 214 inches long, 72.5 inches wide, and 55 inches high.

The Special was 4 inches lower than the K-310 and had a 40-gallon fuel tank. The spare tire was mounted on a tray that could be pulled out for easier access. It was lowered from the rear by using a hydraulic cylinder that could be activated from inside the car. This car also used push-button door latches on the outside and inside.

Power came from a 331-cubic-inch Hemi V-8 and a Fluid Drive automatic transmission.

As with the two earlier cars, the wheel wells were opened to expose the 16-inch wire wheels. The rear fenders were raised to form simple fins and to take away from the drastic slope of the fastback hood. The body was aluminum from the windshield back and steel from the windshield

The 1956 Norseman was one of the most fabled dream cars ever. Built by Ghia, it was lost on the *Andrea Doria* when that ship collided with the *Stockholm* and sank off the coast of Long Island. *Daimler Chrysler Historical Collection*

forward, except for an aluminum hood. It incorporated a flattened grille and melded the front bumper with the grille.

Ghia liked this car so much that Chrysler gave the company permission to build a limited number of production cars based on the design. Called the GS-1 and sold only in Europe, either 50 or 400 were built, depending on the source of information.

1953 Special Modified

This car used the same sheet-metal forms as the Special, and was built on the 125.5-inch-wheelbase New Yorker chassis. Still, the Modified was 10 inches shorter than the Special. Two copies of this car were built, incorporating the K-310 styling features of open wheel wells, sculptured fenders, short rear deck, and long front deck. The Modified also used a reverse hood scoop and cowl intakes and had door handles instead of push buttons. The spare was mounted vertically in the trunk. The Modified also rode on 15-inch wheels instead of the 16-inch wheels of the Special.

1953 D'Elegance

D'Elegance used a horizontal line starting at the front fender and arching up over the rear wheel as a style feature. It also used a sloping rear window and "donut deck" that included a spare-tire impression that actually covered the spare tire for a change. The D'Elegance shared the "microphone taillights" of the K-310 and C-200, and was a two-passenger fastback sport coupe that was built on a shortened

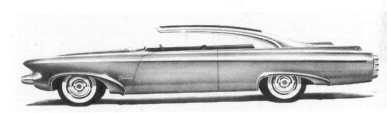

New Yorker chassis. The wheelbase was 115 inches, while the other critical dimensions were 104.5 inches length, 74 inches width, and 54.5 inches height. Power came from a 331-cubic-inch Hemi V-8 rated at 180 horsepower, working through a Fluid Torque automatic transmission.

The front ends of the D'Elegance and the K-310 were similar, with a small grille and bumper below the grille. The headlights were hooded. The rear fenders were heavily

The gas turbine engine that powered the Turboflite was a generation younger than the one used in the 1962 turbine car. But it wasn't the engine that distinguished the Turboflite; it was a tinted glass canopy that raised with the windshield to facilitate entry and exit. Side windows were hinged to the roof. *Daimler Chrysler Historical Collection*

sculpted, and the front fenders were round in front and simply designed.

An interesting story attached to this car was that Volkswagen executives were allowed to see Ghia's sketches of the D'Elegance. At the time, VW was under pressure to come up with a sportier model than the standard Beetle. VW and Ghia took the basic D'Elegance style and reduced it to VW dimensions for the design of the Karmann Ghia sports coupe.

1954 La Comtesse

The "female" version of a pair of New Yorker Deluxe Newports that was modified for the show circuits was the 1954 La Comtesse. Like its "male" counterpart, La Comtesse featured a full-length plexiglass roof section. It was painted pink and had a white vinyl roof in the areas that weren't plexiglass.

1954 Le Comte

The "male" New Yorker Deluxe Sedan was painted bronze with a black roof. It, too, had a color-coordinated interior, wire wheels, and a continental spare tire kit.

1955 Ghia Falcon

One of Virgil Exner's idea cars, the Falcon was built by Ghia, who had a hand in bringing many of Exner's creations to metal. This was a two-passenger roadster built on a 105-inch-wheelbase chassis. Exner noted that the Falcon took its inspiration from jet fighters and boats, which both have pronounced wedge shapes. "The mechanical aspects [of the Falcon] are emphasized in keeping with its likeness to modern competition sports cars," Exner said. "We lent a feeling

of power to the Falcon by means of externally mounted dual exhaust systems and fender louvers." The Falcon had a sloping hood that made it appear to move forward eagerly.

1955 Flight Sweep I

Another of Exner's idea cars, the Flight Sweep I featured dramatic wedge-shaped styling. The rear fenders were swept up into a fin, as with Exner's "Forward Look" production cars. The Flight Sweep I was a low four-passenger hardtop that had its color line begin at the fin and extend forward and gradually upward, ending in front fender extensions that carried beyond the headlights and seemed to lead the car ahead.

1955 Flight Sweep II

This car was identical to the Flight Sweep I, except that it was a convertible and had a different color treatment, although the accent lines were the same.

1956 Norseman

Ghia had designed and built several dream cars for the Chrysler Corporation by the mid-1950s. However, after a couple of less-than-ideal cars coming from Italy, Chrysler began development of its own dream cars. There was one final vehicle, however, and this was one for the ages.

Ghia had built a dream car that was called the Chrysler Norseman. Chrysler placed an estimated value of $200,000 on the car. Chrysler said the Norseman had more structural, chassis, electrical, and styling innovations than any other idea car the company had designed. After Ghia completed the car, it was crated and placed on a new luxury liner on July 17, 1956, for shipment to the United States. That liner was the *Andrea Doria*. On July 26, 1956, nearing the port of New York, the *Andrea Doria* was struck by the Swedish-American Line's *Stockholm*. The hole in the side of the *Andrea Doria* was large and the liner sank, with the Chrysler Norseman in the hold. It was never recovered. The *Stockholm* limped into New York with a crushed bow and the *Andrea Doria*'s passengers lining the rails. The car was covered by insurance.

The Norseman had no pillars or posts on its aluminum body, and it contained a 12-square-foot power glass sun-roof. The roof was supported by structural cantilever arches that curved upward from the rear frame and over the passenger compartment. Like any self-respecting car of 1956, it had upswept tail fins and a sharply sloping hood. The underbody was smooth for aerodynamic efficiency. The grille and front bumpers were in a direct line to permit maximum cooling airflow with minimum aerodynamic drag. The headlights were concealed behind streamlined hoods that opened automatically when the lights were turned on.

There were no vent windows, although most cars of the era used them. In their place were special fresh air vents in the front portion of the roof that contained hidden vanes to control the air intake and eliminate drafts.

Inside there were four individual bucket seats that were power operated for adjustment and comfort. Each had its own set of automatically retracting seat belts. The instrument panel was cushioned with shock absorbent padding, while the instruments themselves were mounted in pods that hung from streamlined struts suspended from the panel. The front passenger had the use of a writing desk that folded down from the instrument panel.

The Norseman was on Chrysler drawing boards for a year and it took another 15 months to build it. The Norseman was 227.5 inches long on a 129-inch wheelbase. It was 80 inches wide and 57 inches tall. Under the hood was a special advanced Chrysler engine that drove the rear wheels through a push-button PowerFlite transmission. The suspension was advanced and, according to Chrysler officials, "represented thousands of hours of laboratory testing."

"Fate has denied the public the opportunity to see the wonders of the Norseman," a Chrysler official said, "but engineers have pulled the drawings and blueprints out of file drawers and are determined that the engineering and styling concepts will be further developed to appear in future cars."

1960 Dart

Designed by Virgil Exner, this idea car had a sloping nose and "bat wing" tailfins that were deemed too radical for its time.

1961 Turboflite

This was introduced in late 1961 and was powered by a gas turbine engine that was a generation younger than the one used in the 1962 turbine car. But it wasn't the engine that distinguished the Turboflite; it was a tinted glass canopy that rose with the windshield to facilitate entry and exit. Side windows were hinged to the roof. Opening the door required pushing a button. After you entered the car and closed the door, the roof would descend. Four red warning lights would flash to warn passengers about the

Called the 300 when it debuted as a dream car, this vehicle would emerge later as the Newport, a sleek four-door sedan with flowing lines. Under the hood was an 8.0-liter V-10 engine with multi-port fuel injection from the Viper parts bin. While no numbers were quoted for the 300, in Viper trim the engine developed 450 horsepower, far more than the 300 horsepower of the title cars. *Daimler Chrysler Historical Collection*

The Atlantic was allegedly suggested by then-Chrysler president Bob Lutz. It was a throwback to such classic designs as the Bugatti Atlantique. Among the design features were a horizontal neon lamp strip, instead of the individual tail lights of the Bugatti, and a softer fastback slope to the rear window. *Daimler Chrysler Historical Collection*

descending roof. In the rear of the Turboflite was a high-mounted wing that acted as an air brake. It would pivot up into the airstream whenever the brakes were applied. The taillamps and turn signals were located behind a single lens that spanned the entire width of the car. The front-end styling was reminiscent of the Cord 810.

1962 Turbine

The "production" Chrysler Turbine was actually the fourth-generation turbine car to come from Chrysler Engineering. A fleet of 55 was built for consumer testing around the country. The Chrysler Turbine looked very much like the 1961-1963 Thunderbird, and rightly so. Elwood Engel, who designed the T-Bird for Ford before he left, also penned the Turbine. With two round headlights, a horizontal grille, and a classic hardtop greenhouse, the Turbine was no stretch of the imagination in design. In the rear was a V-shaped fascia and exhausts that looked as if they had been lifted from a jet plane. It was the engine that was unique, and the flaws in turbine engine design were what kept the car from full production.

Richard M. Langworth and Jan Norbye noted in *A Complete History of the Chrysler Corporation*, "A bucket-seat, four-passenger two-door hardtop, it was painted Turbine Bronze and equipped with full power assists, automatic transmission, and other luxury equipment. Headlight and backup light bezels were styled with a rotary-blade motif to emphasize the car's unusual power source, and there were

massive 'boomerang' horizontal taillights set into steeply angled rear fenders."

Road & Track said it felt that "the unbelievable styling tends to detract from what otherwise is one of the most interesting experiments ever tried by Detroit." Built on a 110-inch wheelbase, the Turbine weighed 3,900 pounds—heavy for its time. Chrysler said the turbine engine developed 130 horsepower and 425 foot-pounds of torque at zero rpm, which was equivalent to 200 brake horsepower in a piston engine. According to Chrysler, it had a top speed of 115 miles per hour and a 0-60-miles-per-hour time of 13.2 seconds. The fuel economy was a disappointing 11.5 miles per gallon.

Among the other interesting features were a rubber-mounted front suspension, new power steering and braking systems, vehicle deceleration using engine braking, and quick throttle response. The engine was connected to a three-speed automatic transmission that didn't use a torque converter because the low-speed torque of the engine made one unnecessary.

1991 300

Called the 300 when it debuted as a dream car, this vehicle would emerge later as the Newport, a sleek four-door sedan with flowing lines. Chrysler promotional literature noted that the 300 was built for one purpose: to be driven. It recalled the legendary "Letter Series" 300 cars of Chrysler's racing past. Under the hood was an 8.0-liter V-10 engine with multi-port fuel injection from the Viper parts bin. While no numbers were quoted for the 300, in Viper trim the engine developed 450 horsepower, far more than the 300 horsepower of the title cars.

The gently sloping hood, flared panels, and rounded boat-tail rear end concealed full ground effects and a speed-actuated spoiler that would provide road-gripping performance.

Inside, all controls were within the driver's reach. Instruments were large rounded gauges that were designed to be read quickly and accurately. The driver's area was trimmed in soft black leather, while the passenger seats were tan leather with touches of wood trim.

The 300 rode on a lengthy 125.9-inch wheelbase, and was 206.5 inches long overall. It was 76.3 inches wide and 51.2 inches high. Twenty-inch wheels and tires put the power to the road in the rear, while the front wheels and tires were 19 inches in diameter.

1995 Atlantic

Allegedly suggested by then-Chrysler President Bob Lutz, the Chrysler Atlantic was a throwback to such classic designs as the Bugatti Atlantique. According to the legend, Lutz, as much an enthusiast of classic cars as of newer models, was having lunch with engineering vice president Francois Castaing and design vice president Tom Gale in 1993 when he sketched his idea for a modern version of the Bugatti on the back of a table napkin. "Wouldn't it be fun if we could build a car like that?" Lutz asked the other two. Gale took the napkin back to the studio and gave it to Jack Crain to flesh out. Bob Hubbach made a 1/5-scale model, then designed the final bodywork. Michael Castiglione designed the interior. The result is remarkably close to Lutz's sketch.

Chrysler introduced the Atlantic at the Detroit Auto Show in January 1995. Interestingly, while the Bugatti Atlantique provided the inspiration for Lutz, Hubbach told Michael Lamm in *Collectible Automobile*, "The Talbot [Lago] probably gave me more cues than the Bugatti."

The final design work was completed at Chrysler Pacifica, the corporation's West Coast design studio, under Kevin Verduyn. Among the final design features were a horizontal neon lamp strip instead of the individual taillights of the Bugatti, and a softer fastback slope to the rear window. Lutz also drew in a spine, but that feature was rejected early in the design process.

The Atlantic was built around a tubular chassis based on the Dodge Viper front and rear ends, which also supplied the independent front and rear suspensions. Power came from a 4.0-liter straight-eight that was created by welding two Neon twin cam four-cylinder engines together with a common crankcase. The straight-eight was chosen because that's what powered the Bugatti Atlantique. It was rated at 325 horsepower and was mated to a four-speed automatic transaxle.

The Atlantic rode on 21- and 22-inch-diameter wheels, front and rear, respectively. The two-plus-two interior was upholstered in cream-colored leather. Instead of using wood for trim—it was too predictable—Chrysler chose to use a man-made maroon cloth that had a woven carbon-fiber look. The instruments had a Swiss watch-type look to them in keeping with the classic theme.

Neil Walling explained to Lamm, "There were a lot of very beautifully proportioned cars and beautiful details done in the past. Designers really do find inspiration in looking at older shapes. I've walked around Concours with Tom Gale, and we've talked about specific fenders of specific cars, the combination of soft and sharp-edged forms from 50 years ago . . . talking about how we could apply that sort of design to projects we're working on in the studios. . . . So to that extent I think we really do miss the boat if we don't look back and only look forward. It's a rich heritage."

The Chrysler Atlantic ended up being 201.7 inches long on a 124.5-inch wheelbase. It was 51.6 inches high and 75.8 inches wide.

The Chrysler LHX was an extension of the LH production car with an even more pronounced cab-forward design and a steeply sloped windshield. LHX emphasized Chrysler's feeling that a family sedan doesn't have to look dull and stodgy. *Daimler Chrysler Historical Collection*

Like the Atlantic, the Phaeton looked back on the glory days of the 1930s and its elegant cars. This four-door, four-seat convertible had a separate windshield for rear-seat passengers. It was powered by a 5.4-liter V-12, which was two 2.7-liter V-6 engines welded together and using a common crankshaft. *Daimler Chrysler Historical Collection*

1996 LHX

Unveiled alongside the Dodge Intrepid ESX at the 1996 North American International Auto show in Detroit, the Chrysler LHX was an extension of the LH production car with an even more pronounced cab-forward design and a steeply sloped windshield. The LHX emphasized Chrysler's feeling that family sedans don't have to look dull and stodgy.

1997 Phaeton

Like the Atlantic, the Phaeton looked back on the glory days of the 1930s and its elegant cars. This four-door, four-seat convertible had a separate windshield for rear-seat passengers. It was powered by a 5.4-liter V-12, which was two 2.7-liter V-6 engines welded together and using a common crankshaft.

The Phaeton was inspired by the 1940 Newport parade car. "With this car, we expanded the use of today's convertible by giving it four doors and two windshields," said Chrysler Corporation Design Director Neil Walling. The Phaeton was painted a two-tone Champagne Pearl with machine-polished wheels and trim. Details gave the car a coach-built quality, with an egg-crate grille; retractable rear compartment windshield; and an interior that included cream-and-brown-colored leather trim, woven cream leather inserts, satin metal details, and Zebrano wood accents.

Both front and rear compartments were separate and had their own radio, climate controls, and luxurious seats, arm rests, and center consoles. The speedometer and tachometer gauges were also included in both compartments.

The Phaeton was 215.0 inches long, built on a 132.0-inch wheelbase. It was 78.0 inches wide and 55.0 inches tall. The tires were P245/55R22 Goodyears, mounted on 8x22 cast-aluminum wheels.

Daimler Chrysler Historical Collection

Above and Below. The four-door Chronos was another Chrysler look into the future. Chronos was 17 feet long and was powered by the Viper V-10 engine, detuned to 350 horsepower. It used a four-speed electronic automatic transmission. *Daimler Chrysler Historical Collection*

1998 Chronos

The four-door Chronos was another Chrysler look into the future. The Chronos was 17 feet long and was powered by the Viper V-10 engine, detuned to 350 horsepower. It used a four-speed electronic automatic transmission. The rear wheels were 21 inches in diameter and the fronts 20 inches in diameter. Chrysler Chief of Design John Herlitz said he thought the Chronos was the right vehicle to serve as a flagship vehicle for Chrysler. With a profile similar to that of the Atlantic, the Chronos had no exterior door handles.

"We've been looking for years at the possibility of finding the right product for a Chrysler flagship model," Herlitz said. "This time we may have struck all the right chords."

The wheels integrated smoothly with the side surface of the car to give it a solid stance. With the wheels pushed forward and aft and the cabin shifted rearward, the Chronos had the proportions of some of the Virgil Exner classics. The surface flowed cleanly from the large front grille and jewel-like headlamps, to the steeply raked windshield and the short rear deck, which was highlighted by perfectly placed creases to give the body definition. Crisp creases ran from both A-pillars to the front of the car and along the sides, giving subtle highlights and shadows to the sterling-blue clear coat paint.

Inside, the hand-wrapped leather steering wheel and hand-sewn leather center console and door trim panels showed the meticulous attention given to the Chronos, which reminded viewers of the same attention to detail offered by early coachbuilders. White-faced instruments sat in wood dash panels, again echoing the handcrafted era of luxury cars. The center console also featured an in-place cigar humidor, with storage, lighter, and hygrometer.

The suspension used short long-arms front and rear. Combined with the unitized body structure and isolated

front and rear subframes and high-strength steel chassis, the Chronos was highly spirited and balanced. The Chronos was 205.4 inches long, 76.5 inches wide, and 52.7 inches tall, with a curb weight of 4,200 pounds.

1998 CCV

CCV stands for Composite Concept Vehicle, and the CCV was Chrysler's study into using thermoplastic glass-reinforced composite materials in the panels of a vehicle. With a body that looked surprisingly like a Citroen 2CV, the CCV was right-hand drive, light in weight, and economical to produce.

1999 Citadel

Chrysler called the Citadel "a new breed of crossover vehicle that provided the driving passion of the Chrysler 300M and ample cargo room." The Citadel was not only a

Above and Below. The Citadel was a crossover vehicle that provided the driving passion of the Chrysler 300M with ample cargo room. Citadel also had a hybrid powertrain. One power source was a 3.5-liter V-6 gasoline engine that developed 235 horsepower and drove the rear wheels. The front wheels were driven by two Siemens Automotive electric motors, adding 70 horsepower to the mix. *Daimler Chrysler Historical Collection*

styling hybrid, it also had a hybrid powertrain. One power source was a 3.5-liter V-6 gasoline engine that developed 235 horsepower and drove the rear wheels. The front wheels were driven by two Siemens Automotive electric motors, adding 70 horsepower to the mix. The hybrid mix was used to recover energy normally lost when braking, while providing all-wheel drive without the complexities of a more conventional parallel hybrid.

Among the Citadel's other features were dual-power sliding rear doors and a retracting cargo door that slid under the floor. Built on the Concorde platform, it was 192 inches long, 75 inches wide, and 59 inches tall. The 125-inch wheelbase was longer than the Concorde's, primarily to accommodate rear-wheel drive, and it had 2 inches more ground clearance. It was also 3 inches taller and had 1.3 cubic feet additional storage space.

"We wanted to make it easy for a wheelchair-bound driver to get in and out of the driver's seat," said Neil Walling,

DaimlerChrysler's vice president for Advanced Design. "We've done a pretty good job, I'm told, with full-size vans for the physically challenged. Why not give the disabled driver or passenger the option of a stylish crossover vehicle?"

The Citadel was green with a tan and green leather interior. It was designed by Osamu Shikado, who also designed the exterior of the 1998 Chrysler Chronos concept car.

1999 Pacifica

From the corporation that invented the minivan came three innovations in 1999 that stretched the envelope of minivan design and practicality. Chrysler's contribution to the mix was the Pacifica, which moved minivan luxury to new heights.

"Our Pacifica concept minivan was inspired by the luxury and convenience offered in executive jet travel," said Neil Walling. "We wanted Pacifica to bring benefits of executive jet travel down to earth, into the minivan and on to the road."

Consequently, rear passengers in this 119.3-inch-wheelbase minivan were treated to two fully reclining, adjustable power leather seats with power foot rests, similar to those offered in a first-class luxury aircraft. Six-passenger seating was accomplished with two jump seats and a split-bench 50/50 seat configuration. The interior came complete with airline-inspired overhead storage bins, overhead lighting, drop-down video screen, and woodgrain accents.

In addition, the Pacifica had two skylights that ran the length of the roof. "The sky lights are used to create an open, architectural feel inside," Walling added. "We wanted passengers to feel like they were in their family room or some other special place."

The raised roof provided space for the overhead storage bins and a separate passenger-side exterior storage compart-

Above and Below. Pacifica was one of three 1999 minivan innovations that stretched the envelope of minivan design and practicality. Chrysler's contribution to the mix was the Pacifica, which moved minivan luxury to new heights. Rear passengers in this 119.3-inch-wheelbase minivan were treated to two fully reclining, adjustable power leather seats with power foot rests, similar to those offered in a first-class luxury aircraft. *Daimler Chrysler Historical Collection*

ment that was ideal for storing wet skis or golf umbrellas. A special golf bag rack system was built into the rear of the cabin that allowed storage for up to four sets of clubs.

The overall dimensions included a length of 200.7 inches, a width of 76.3 inches, and a height of 74.1 inches. Power came from a 180-horsepower 3.8-liter V-6.

1999 Java

Introduced at the Frankfurt International Automobile Show, the Chrysler Java was intended to be a fresh approach at an important European market segment. The Java made maximum use of its exterior dimensions by incorporating a "one box" design profile. Tom Gale said he thought the Java "moved cab-forward design to the next level. This show car features what we call 'Passenger Priority Design' with tall architecture and panoramic seating for the driver and passengers, allowing higher H-points (hip points) to give them more of an in-control feeling compared to other small cars. The rear passengers sit higher than the front passengers, creating an automotive form of theatre seating."

With a single low egg-crate grille to attach it to Chrysler heritage, the Java was built on a 98.3-inch wheelbase and had a 59.1-inch front track and a 58.7-inch rear track. Tall upright taillamps provided a unique rear signature and maximum visibility in congested European city traffic. The exterior design was rounded off by prominent detailed headlamps, taut body side surfacing, and large mechanically inspired 18-inch wheels.

The interior was inspired by Swedish furniture showrooms, with light colors and materials. Featured were brushed aluminum, chrome, cream and light green leather, and curly maple wood. The gauge cluster had a unique three-dimensional execution.

The Java was powered by an 80-horsepower, 1.4-liter four-cylinder engine mated to a five-speed manual transmission. The front suspension incorporated wishbones, MacPherson struts, double-tube shock absorbers, and a torsion bar stabilizer. Trailing links with coil springs with single-tube shock absorbers and a torsion bar stabilizer made up the rear suspension.

CHAPTER 5

Dodge

With Virgil Exner choosing Plymouth as his preferred design brand, Dodge often found itself overshadowed by its less-expensive brother, at least when it came to dream cars. But the company founded by the Dodge brothers did have a few unique dream cars in the 1950s and 1960s that were "knock your socks off" different.

In 1953 and 1954, there was a series of Firearrow cars that were drop-dead gorgeous. The Flitewing of 1962 was innovative. More-modern cars like the 1991 Neon and 1996 Intrepid ESX2 were close to production. And, of course, we can't forget that the Viper began as a dream car. So will the Copperhead (now known as Dodge Concept Car) be far behind?

In recent years, Dodge has chosen to honor past notable Dodge models with modern variations, such as the Charger R/T and the Power Wagon pickup. With these two models, Dodge pays homage to its past while keeping an eye on the future.

1953 Firearrow Roadster

The Firearrow, introduced in 1953, was a sport roadster built on a 115-inch-wheelbase chassis. The car was designed by Virgil Exner and built by Ghia in Italy. Extremely low at the cowl, the Firearrow only measured 46.25 inches tall at the top of the windshield. Despite the low height, road clearance was only 2 inches less than a production Dodge. Its aspect ratio was excellent, with a width more than twice its height.

The Firearrow featured an oval grille bisected by a horizontal chrome bumper. This bumper wrapped completely around the car and extended back to the rear of the rear fenders. Quad headlights were mounted below the bumper. Unlike some other cars of the era, the wheels were not fully cut out and had a slight flat section at the top. Inside, the upholstery in this two-seater was leather, while the steering wheel was of polished wood with aluminum spokes.

The Firearrow was 188.8 inches long and 75.5 inches wide. This first Firearrow was a body mockup only and had no powerplant. The 1954 Firearrow, on the other hand, was a complete car.

1954 Firearrow Roadster

This version of the Firearrow sported a 241.3-cubic-inch V-8 engine that developed 150 horsepower. It drove the rear wheels through a PowerFlite automatic transmission. Like the original, the windshield was unframed and had no header. It first appeared at the "Harmony on Wheels" show.

This version of the Firearrow retained the same dramatic styling as the original with some minor changes. For example, the grille was now rectangular with rounded corners. It was still bisected by a horizontal bumper that extended around the car to the rear fenders, but the bumper

The Firearrow was a 34-inch-high sport roadster built on a 115-inch-wheelbase chassis. The car was designed by Virgil Exner and built by Ghia in Italy. Despite the low height, road clearance was only two inches less than a production Dodge. Its aspect ratio was excellent, with a width more than twice its height. *Daimler Chrysler Historical Collection*

The second version of the Firearrow sported a 241.3-cubic inch V-8 engine that developed 150 horsepower, unlike the previous version, which had no engine. It drove the rear wheels through a PowerFlite automatic transmission. Like the original, the windshield was unframed and had no header. *Daimler Chrysler Historical Collection*

The Firearrow Sport Coupe was shorter than the Roadster at 190.6 inches, slightly wider at 76.5 inches and considerably taller at 55.0 inches. The Firearrow Sport Coupe retained the same basic shape and styling features as the second Firearrow Roadster, but it had a permanent hardtop with a notched back. *Daimler Chrysler Historical Collection*

Dodge's third of three Firearrow dream cars for 1954 was the Firearrow convertible. It shared the same design features as the second Sport Roadster and the Sport Coupe but with a convertible top. Again, the flat-top wheel cutouts exposed chrome wire wheels. *Daimler Chrysler Historical Collection*

also passed through single headlights at each side. The squared-off wheel openings displayed chrome wire wheels, unlike the disc wheels of its predecessor.

The Firearrow was built on a 119.0-inch wheelbase and was 194.0 inches long overall, 50.9 inches tall, and 76.3 inches wide.

1954 Firearrow Sport Coupe

Built on the same 119.0-inch wheelbase as the second Firearrow Roadster, the Sport Coupe was shorter at 190.6 inches, slightly wider at 76.5 inches, and considerably taller at 55.0 inches. The Firearrow Sport Coupe retained the same basic shape and styling features as the second Firearrow Roadster, but it had a permanent hardtop with a notched back. The engine and transmission were also the same as in the second Roadster. In addition, the front end was cleaned up and the grille added a concave "waterfall" feature with 17 vertical chrome slats. It was a car that would go, and reached 143.44 miles per hour on the banked oval at Chrysler's proving grounds.

1954 Firearrow Convertible

Dodge's third of three Firearrow dream cars for 1954 was the Firearrow Convertible. It shared the same design features as the second Roadster and the Sport Coupe, but with a convertible top (the Roadster had no top). Again, the flat-top wheel cutouts exposed chrome wire wheels. The grille was changed again for this car and now sported an egg-crate design. Under the hood was the same 241.3-cubic-inch V-8 as in the other cars, rated at 150 horsepower. It was connected to a PowerFlite transmission.

Inside, the upholstery was in a harlequin-checked leather. The rear seat was a bench while the front seats were

The Flitewing had a body that, according to Dodge, "exemplifies the aerodynamic closed sports car." Like the Chrysler Turboflite that was also introduced that year, the Flitewing had windows that rose like gullwing doors to aid entry. Each window would rise to a position over the door whenever the door handle was moved and would descend automatically when the door was closed. *Daimler Chrysler Historical Collection*

basic buckets. This car is credited with inspiring the limited-production Dual-Ghia sports car.

1962 Flitewing

According to Dodge, the Flitewing had a body that "exemplifies the aerodynamic closed sports car." Like the Chrysler Turboflite that was also introduced that year, the Flitewing had windows that rose like gullwing doors to aid entry. Each window would rise to a position over the door whenever the door handle was moved and would descend automatically when the door was closed. The instrumentation on the Flitewing was also unique. The speedometer showed speed in a series of 13 oval windows that would light up in 10-miles-per-hour increments. Accessory equipment

The 1991 Neon was the precursor to the production version of the compact car. Unlike the production version, though, the dream car used a 1.1-liter two-stroke three-cylinder engine that produced 100 horsepower. Styling reflected current Dodge themes with cab-forward design, a sharply inclined hood and windshield, and an integrated rear spoiler. *Daimler Chrysler Historical Collection*

Dodge already had a production car called the Intrepid when it introduced the Intrepid ESX2 in 1996 at the Detroit Auto Show. This car was among the first of Chrysler Corporation's cab-forward designs that increased interior space without increasing the size of the automobile. The ESX2 also used a hybrid diesel/electric powerplant that did not appear on the production version. *Daimler Chrysler Historical Collection*

such as the turn signals, light, and power antenna switches were located on the driver's door.

The Flitewing was powered by a 383-cubic-inch Wedge V-8 that developed 330 horsepower.

1991 Neon

The 1991 Neon was the precursor to the production version of the compact car. Unlike the production version, though, the dream car used a 1.1-liter two-stroke three-cylinder engine that produced 100 horsepower. The styling reflected current Dodge themes with cab-forward design, a sharply inclined hood and windshield, and an integrated

rear spoiler. Cab-forward styling maximized interior space and maintained mechanical space. The Neon was a full five-passenger sedan.

In front of the driver was a cluster of analog gauges. All of the seats were removable for easy cleaning, as were the stereo and headrest speakers. The Neon also had a fabric roof that could be folded back for maximum sun and air.

This Neon was 167.7 inches long on a 104.0-inch wheelbase. It was 66.5 inches wide and 57.2 inches tall, riding on 17-inch wheels and tires.

The Neon concept car won the 1991 Gold Industrial Design Excellence Award (IDEA) from the Industrial Designers Society of America for its "refreshing design with content and thoroughness unusual for a show car."

1996 Intrepid ESX2

Dodge already had a production car called the Intrepid when it introduced this concept car in 1996 at the Detroit Auto Show. This car was among the first of Chrysler Corporation's cab-forward designs that increased interior space without increasing the size of the automobile.

The 1996 Intrepid ESX2 showed what direction a new edition of the car might go. In fact, the dream car was an accurate predictor of the production car. However, the ESX2 also used a hybrid diesel/electric powerplant that did not appear on the production version. The ESX2 had an all-aluminum body, and Chrysler was not yet ready to use all-aluminum bodies on its high-volume vehicles.

In the back of the ESX2 was a 1.8-liter diesel engine that didn't power the wheels. Rather, the diesel charged a bank of 150 small electric batteries that in turn powered two 100-brake horsepower Zytek electric motors that were also rear mounted. The batteries themselves weighed 180 pounds and developed 90 kilowatts. While the Intrepid ESX2 could

This car began life as the Copperhead, but legal problems in 1999 forced the car to be renamed the Dodge Concept Car. Created in the spirit of the Austin-Healey 3000, the "Concept Car" used a 2.7-liter DOHC V-6 rated at 220 horsepower. The open two-seat sports car was painted in Copper Fire Orange, a color that was intended to make it visible at night. *Daimler Chrysler Historical Collection*

reach 50 miles per hour, the batteries' inability to deliver power for an extended period of time was their drawback.

The ESX2 was also computer friendly. Chrysler developed a docking station to connect a Windows CE hand-held PC directly to the car, rather than implement an on-board system that could become obsolete. The computer could then access the Internet for e-mail, maps, and weather reports. It would also check vehicle diagnostics, dial the onboard telephone, and turn on lights and security systems in the owner's home.

The ESX2 was 195 inches long on a 113-inch wheelbase. It was 76 inches wide, 52.6 inches tall, and rode on 19-inch front tires and 20-inch rear tires. Four-wheel disc brakes also used regenerative braking of the electric motors.

1996 Ram T-Rex

A macho version of the Ram pickup, the T-Rex sported six wheels, a bed-mounted roll bar, and an array of four fog lights across the roof. It was designed not so much to be practical as to intimidate other drivers on the road, off the road, and in towing just about anything.

1996 Caravan ESS

An extension of Dodge's Caravan minivan, the Caravan ESS was a special model designed to accommodate varied lifestyles and needs. It took the standard Caravan ES and Sport models to a new level with its eye-catching Torch Red exterior and aggressive styling. Among the new and unique performance styling cues were a honeycombed textured grille, a lower fascia with prominent fog lamps, unique side cladding, badging, and graphics, and a rear fascia and spoiler.

The interior reflected the all-out performance theme with a sleek, molded instrument panel that had carbon-fiber appliqués. Perforated leather bucket seats provided seating

The Sidewinder Dream Truck combined features of the Ram with the Viper, including the Viper's 600 horsepower V-10 engine. *Daimler Chrysler Historical Collection*

for six, with lateral support to hold the driver and the other five passengers in place.

Under the hood was a high-performance 3.8-liter V-6 engine rated at 215 horsepower. An AutoStick transaxle that combined an automatic with a clutchless manual got the power to the front wheels. The front and rear suspensions were also modified to make the most of Caravan's wide stance. Goodyear 225/50R18 performance tires completed the package, along with four-wheel disc brakes and ABS.

The Caravan ESS was 186.3 inches long on a 113.3-inch wheelbase. It was 75.6 inches wide and 68.5 inches high.

1997 Concept Car

This car began life as the Copperhead, but legal problems in 1999 forced the car to be renamed the Dodge Concept Car. It's a rather unromantic name for an exciting car, but DaimlerChrysler has asked us to comply. So, here's the Dodge Concept Car.

Like the Viper before it that was the hit of the 1993 Detroit Auto Show, the "Concept Car" starred at the 1997 show. Created in the spirit of the Austin-Healey 3000, the Concept Car used a 2.7-liter DOHC V-6 rated at 220 horsepower. This was unlike the Viper's massive 8.0-liter V-10. The gearbox was a five-speed manual affair. The Concept Car used a fully independent suspension with semi-trailing wishbones in the front and rear. The ground clearance was 5 inches.

Chrysler Design Director Neil Walling said, "We designed [Concept Car] to look fast by utilizing minimum overhang and pushing the wheels out to the front and rear corners." The open two-seat sports car was painted in Copper Fire Orange, a color that was intended to make it visible, apparently, at night. The interior used black snakeskinlike leather with red piping to further enhance the Austin-Healey image. The tires even had a snakeskin tread pattern. All the instruments were clustered in a center pod, except for the tachometer, which was directly in front of the driver.

The Concept Car's sleek dimensions were achieved by pushing the wheels to the limits of the vehicle's frame, and then adding 18-inch wheels in the front and 20-inch wheels in the rear. An air scoop grille, deep-set quad headlamps, elongated hood with dual air scoops, drastically sloped windshield, and scaled-down dorsal fin on the rear deck lid contributed to the Concept Car's sinuous feel.

1997 Sidewinder

This dream truck combined features of the Ram with the Viper. From the Viper came the 600 horsepower V-10 engine; from the Ram came durability. The Sidewinder also

The four-door Charger R/T was powered by a supercharged compressed natural gas (CNG) 4.7-liter V-8 engine that generated 325 horsepower. In addition to the four doors, which distinguished it from the production R/T, the Charger R/T also used a new fuel storage system. *Daimler Chrysler Historical Collection*

Dodge Caravan R/T added performance to the minivan equation, including 18-inch wheels, an AutoStick transaxle, rear spoiler, and a 225 horsepower 3.5-liter V-6 aluminum block multi-valve V-6 engine. *John Heilig*

had a chassis based on Trans Am racers and had styling cues that included the Viper's disconnect behind the doors.

1999 Caravan R/T minivan

Rather than be content with a minivan reputation that has the vehicles driven by "soccer moms," the Dodge Caravan R/T added performance to the equation. The Caravan R/T added 18-inch wheels, an AutoStick transaxle, rear spoiler, and a 225-horsepower 3.5-liter V-6 aluminum-block multi-valve V-6 engine. Its estimated selling price would be between $20,000 and $30,000, the most popular range for minivan buyers.

"The Dodge image is bold, powerful and capable," said Dodge Division Vice President Jim Julow. "R/T represents the next level of performance, and we use R/T to communicate enhanced performance packages for our vehicles. Dodge Caravan R/T is a concept that explores how R/T distinction might be applied to a minivan."

Painted in Radiant Viper Red, the Caravan R/T was instantly recognizable as a Dodge with its bold, offset grille. Fog lamps and Dodge's distinctive crosshair design were integrated into the vehicle's lower front fascia. Two Viper-style hood scoops, a rear spoiler, and a chrome exhaust tip add to the vehicle's aggressive appearance.

The Viper influence continued inside with a brushed-aluminum instrument panel and racing accelerator and brake pedal. The steering wheel was wrapped in Viper Black leather with Viper Red, Black, and Silver stitching. Seats were Viper Black leather with a red R/T logo embroidered into each headrest.

The Caravan R/T was built on a short 113.3-inch wheelbase, and is 186.3 inches long, 76.8 inches wide, and 68.5 inches tall.

1999 Charger R/T

The four-door Charger R/T was powered by a supercharged compressed natural gas (CNG) 4.7-liter V-8 engine that generated 325 horsepower. In addition to the four doors, which distinguished it from the production R/T, the Charger R/T also used a new fuel storage system that had the possibility of delivering a 300-mile range without compromising trunk space.

The Charger R/T used a new design in gas storage cylinders. Pressure cells inside the storage tank were lined with a gas-impermeable HDPE thermoplastic and wrapped in a hybrid mix of high-strength carbon and glass filaments wound with epoxy resin. The cylinders were laid into a "foam egg crate" to absorb impacts. The fuel cells could be manufactured flat or in the shape of a conventional gas tank. In either shape, they were capable of storing gas at 3,600 psi.

Joe Dehner, responsible for the exterior design, said he felt the Charger R/T concept had just the right "mean streak" to complement its performance features and V-8 power.

"It has muscular lines that are more exaggerated because of the package, with big offset shoulders over the rear wheels," Dehner said. "This Charger R/T has a menacing look to the front end, low and wide, and a powerful-looking rear end. Some aspects remind me of the Dodge Viper. The original Charger had two non-functional scoops stamped into its hood, whereas we have one real scoop at the leading edge of the forward-hinging hood, closest to the front grille."

Interior designer Lance Wagner said he felt the interior resembled a sophisticated fighter-plane cockpit. The pistol grip shifter knob, for example, resembled a fighter's joystick, and the instrument panel was clustered toward the driver, with the tachometer being the dominant gauge.

"That cockpit look is balanced with some late 1960s cues," Wagner said, "such as the big rotary radio dials, the three-spoke steering wheel, and the R/T badge over the glove compartment."

1999 Power Wagon

The Dodge Power Wagon brought back memories of the original postwar model. It was taller than the original at 77 inches, and 3 inches taller than the contemporary Dodge Ram, aided by large-diameter tires. Under the hood was a 7.2-liter direct-injection inline six-cylinder turbocharged diesel engine that developed 780 foot-pounds of torque. The contemporary Ram's 8.0-liter V-10 developed 450 foot-pounds.

"Our objective was to create more of a 'Sharper Image' truck than an everyday work truck," said Trevor Creed, vice president, Advanced Design and Exterior Jeep/Truck, Interior Design, Color & Trim. "With this concept, we're asking 'Is there room in the truck market for appeal to new customers who desire all their extras and still want the traditional capabilities of a truck to pull their boat and haul stuff?'"

Dodge emphasized the development of clean diesel fuels in the introduction of the Power Wagon.

The Dodge Power Wagon resurrected memories of the original postwar model. It was taller than the original at 77 inches, and 3 inches taller than the contemporary Dodge Ram, aided by large-diameter tires. Under the hood was a 7.2-liter direct injection inline six-cylinder turbocharged diesel engine that developed 780 lb-ft of torque. *Daimler Chrysler Historical Collection*

DaimlerChrysler worked with Tulsa-based Syntholeum Corp. to test a new sulfur-free "designer" fuel synthesized from natural gas.

To qualify as a "Super Truck," the Power Wagon rode on 35-inch tires. It weighed 5,357 pounds. Other critical dimensions were a 138.7-inch wheelbase, 207-inch overall length, and 79.9-inch overall width.

The exterior styling was highlighted by the huge tires and six side vents. Up front there were gas-discharge projector-beam headlights. To make loading in the rear easier, there was a power-actuated tailgate. The bed was wood-lined.

"While we were working on the clay model, we brought a red 1946 Power Wagon into the studio," said Mark Allen, the Power Wagon's exterior designer. "From the pictures, we thought it was humungous, but it was dwarfed when we placed it next to the 1999 concept."

The interior styling was not unlike the Audi TT with a combination of leather, brushed aluminum, European ash wood, and steel. The instruments were arrayed in a unique circular display in front of the driver.

"People will have to stretch their imaginations to find similarities between the interior of this Power Wagon and the 1946 original," said interior designer Steve Sowinski. "Whereas the original was a study in raw steel, we used a mix of new materials to get a clean, high-tech look."

The Power Wagon had a winch on the front bumper with enough power to pull an 18-wheeler out of a ditch.

Entry into the Power Wagon was not for mini-skirted girls or senior citizens. It required a step up of nearly 2 feet to reach the running boards and then another foot to enter the cab.

Ford

In 1963, the Ford Motor Company published a book describing the company's philosophy regarding automotive design. *The Ford Book of Styling* was similar to one put out by the GM Design Department in 1938. Several statements from that publication are still important regarding the development of style in production as well as dream cars.

So overwhelming was the novelty of the first automobiles that appearance scarcely mattered.

Despite the preoccupation of most car-builders with the competitive advantages of such radical devices as the self-starter and four-wheel brakes, there were a few who pondered the automobile's potential as a thing of beauty.

In 1927, Edsel Ford organized a styling group. The 1929 Model A was the result.

All styling, by its very nature, is done with an eye to the future. In an isolated area of the Corporate Projects Studio of Ford Motor Company, the stylists most privileged to let imagination roam free work with the distant future in mind. Some develop design ideas that could be suitable for production in four or five years. New engineering features must be anticipated and allowance for their development must be made in these advanced design activities. Large or small cars, sports cars and family cars and commercial vehicles— styling for the future is a constantly exciting challenge. From these explorations often come the first styling themes to be considered for specific model programs. Less inhibited by the demands of production, others dream of cars that will float and fly, or run on energy from a laser beam, or travel close to the ground without wheels. Such research may border on the fantastic, but so did the idea of a carriage going around the country without a horse.

1951 X-100

In *Collectible Automobile*, Joe Oros described the genesis of the Ford X-100:

When George Walker joined Ford the second time around, he was given large flexibility. He was supposed to make recommendations across the board on all products at Ford Motor, cars and trucks. He named Elwood Engel and me as his team on cars and trucks: Elwood, Lincoln-Mercury; Joe, Ford car and truck. We dovetailed with Walker.

The X-100 was done shortly after we went back as consultants for the second time. This was a George Walker project done at Ford. Elwood was the staff assistant for Lincoln-Mercury, so he had little to do with the aesthetic development of the X-100. During the X-100's development, some thought was given to it as a Lincoln Continental, which never went very far. Basically, my responsibility was to bird-dog this design through from start to finish as the first show car from Ford Motor Company. The reason we got started on this car was that I talked to Walker and said, "George, you know if we don't come out with the big rocket tubes on a Ford show car, GM is going to beat us to the punch. I am sure they are going to come out with something like that. It's a natural, I'd say, for them to do that."

Gil Spear was a designer recruited from GM, and was in change of advanced design at Ford. He had made some

Originally, the X-100 was going to be the new Lincoln Continental, but that idea was soon dropped. Ford undertook the "rocket tube" design to beat GM to the punch. *Ford Historical Collection*

George Walker was head of styling at Ford Motor Company when the first dream cars were developed in the early 1950s. Walker was given flexibility at the time to make recommendations for all Ford products. *Ford Historical Collection*

quarter-size scale models of this kind of a theme with the rocket tubes. I said to Walker, "George, Gil Spear has made some models in this vein. If GM were to come out with a show car in this design vein, then we at Ford may have a difficult time to 'lunch' off it." So George said, "Why don't you start it?" We started the X-100.

We then did sketches, and then a full-sized car, and it ended up as a running car, which is now in the Henry Ford Museum. A lot of the show cars have been destroyed, but this one is still there. It came out in early 1952. This car had a tremendous influence on a lot of Ford designs in the Fifties and Sixties.

For example, the X100's canted blades and round taillights suggested much of the design of the 1961-1963 Thunderbird.

The X-100 used a specially designed 300-horsepower high-compression overhead valve V-8 engine. Built on a 123-inch wheelbase, the steel and aluminum body was 220.9 inches long overall, 56.9 inches high, and 81.25 inches wide. It would seat five. The power-operated hood and rear deck lid were opened, closed, locked, and unlocked by controls on the instrument panel. It featured an independent front and rear suspension. Electrically operated jacks were built into each wheel. The X-100 was a technological marvel, with 24 electric motors, 44 electronic tubes, 50 bulbs, and 92 switches.

1953 X-500

Rumored to be the prototype for the next-generation Lincoln Continental, the X-500 featured "Frenched" headlights with "eyebrows," integral grilles and bumpers, and a long flowing line from the front to the rear. The X-500 had

Like many cars of the era, the 1955 Mystere was powered by a rear-mounted gas turbine. It had a huge lift-up windshield. Clear bubble tops and aircraft-inspired designs were very much in vogue throughout the industry. *Ford Historical Collection*

DePaola was another 3/8-model Ford dream car that represented a way to combine sports car performance with certain features adaptable for use in mass-produced passenger cars. Fairings around the wheel housings represent a unique use of sculptured metal in the lower body. *Ford Historical Collection*

a front end that resembled a Studebaker President, and two "jet exhaust" taillights that looked like a cross between a Chrysler Turbine and a Ford Thunderbird.

1953 Syrtis

This was the definitive "hardtop convertible" that was introduced by Ford when the car company opened its new Research and Engineering Center in Dearborn, Michigan. Syrtis had an all-steel roof that could be lowered electrically under the rear deck lid without interfering with the luggage space. The concept of the hardtop convertible would reach production in the 1957 Ford Skyliner. The Syrtis also had quad exhausts that exited under the doors and skirts over the rear wheels. The general shape of the Syrtis would be echoed in the 1961-1963 Thunderbird.

1955 Mystere

Mystere was powered by a rear-mounted gas turbine. It had a huge lift-up windshield. Joe Oros described the Mystere in *Collectible Automobile*.

There were a lot of design themes at the time that were picked up by both the Mystere and the production models. In the various studios, the designers were busy with production design and advance design. Some of the advance thinking of clear bubble tops and aircraft-inspired designs were very much in vogue—not only at Ford Motor, but also throughout the industry. Fins as well were being used in automobile design, straight as well as canted. Bill Boyer at the time had a lot to do with the Mystere-show-car development. The executive designer of the project was Bob Maguire and the chief designer was Frank Hershey.

The Mystere had an effect on the design development of the Fifties cars, and particularly the '57 Fairlane 500. Now

when you look at the back end of the Mystere photograph, it shows a giant exhaust pipe combo taillight bumper. The giant fin of the Mystere comes off of it. On the '57 Ford, that is not the case.

The Mystere had a very low hood between two protruding pod-like fenders with pod lights in them, and it had an elliptical pod bumper underneath the headlight pods with a low hood intake grille. The X-100's low hood and low bumper grille precedes the Mystere's low-hood, low-grille appearance.

When the Mystere was done it was a very fine show car, and it still is. It was right for its time.

1958 Nucleon, La Galaxie, Volante, De Paolo, X-1000, La Tosca

For 1958, Ford designers introduced six 3/8 models of dream cars. These cars were truly dream cars because they often had no designated means of propulsion or even a potential means.

La Tosca was a remote-controlled model that could travel at a speed of five miles per hour and could be controlled at distances of up to 1-1/2 miles. It had a removable fiberglass body. *Ford Historical Collection*

The two-wheeled Gyron was a 3/8-scale model that ran on two wheels but had two additional "training wheels" for when the gyro was switched off. Gyron had automatic computer controls that would allow the driver to sit back and watch the road ahead on an infrared screen. *Ford Historical Collection*

tern, which would provide both lift and thrust. The forward unit is composed of two counterrotating blades and a motor, while each of the two rear units is made up of a single set of blades moving in opposite directions to offset torque."

The De Paolo represented one avenue of exploration into the development of a vehicle with both sports car performance and certain features adaptable for use in mass-produced passenger cars. "Its high action styling," Ford said, "is almost an inversion of the form most typical of American automotive styling. Side molding treatment is effected in such a way that it transmits the feeling of motion conveyed by the wheels, while the fairings around the wheel housings represent a unique use of sculptured metal in the lower body."

The influence of supersonic aeronautical design was evident in the X-1000 with its bubble-type canopy, delta-shaped fins, and suspended jet-pod fenders with headlights designed aerodynamically into the fender surfaces. The long torpedo-shaped taillights cantilevered off the inboard surfaces of the tail fin could have enclosed electronic devices to warn of approaching vehicles. A push-button control and the instrument panel "float" in the center of the deep-dish safety steering wheel.

The La Tosca was a remote-controlled model that could travel at a speed of five miles per hour and could be controlled

Of course the Nucleon had no powerplant. It was designed to run on nuclear power, and no such engine had yet been developed. None ever would, nor would one be practical because of the amount of shielding necessary to protect the driver and passengers. The Nucleon recognized the necessity of separating the passengers and the powerplant by locating the mock-up engine at the extreme rear of the vehicle, between two beams. This extreme rear weight was somewhat counterbalanced by an equally extreme front overhang. As Jim Hockenhull wrote in *Automobile Quarterly,* "The twin-boom configuration was a neat way to indicate the 'otherness' of an atomic power capsule." Ford's Product Planning and Design staff issued a press release stating that "cars such as the Nucleon illustrate the extent to which research into the future is conducted at the Ford Motor Company."

The La Galaxie's shrouded look offered a marked departure from the appearance of contemporary American cars, according to a Ford brochure. Normal offsets between glass and sheet metal areas were eliminated so that all window glass in the La Galaxie was nearly flush with the sides of the car and with the roof.

The La Galaxie was developed to explore future styling concepts as they evolved from engineering and technological developments. Chief among its features was a proximity warning device that would not only warn of vehicles or objects ahead, it would also stop the car automatically if the driver failed to take action. A screen located in front of the driver would indicate the distance between his vehicle and any other object immediately in front of it.

The interior of the La Galaxie had three fully adjustable and individual front seats. Each had an adjustable headrest and the two outboard seats were also provided with armrests. The rear seat was form-flowed, integrated with the side panels, and accommodated three passengers.

Ford's Volante indicated the direction that the styling of an aero-car might take. According to Ford, "the car might be powered by means of three units arranged in a triangular pat-

Mustang I was a mid-engine two-seat sports car developed by Englishman Roy Lunn and engineer Frank Theyleg. They used the German Ford Taunus 1.5-liter V-4 engine with a midship mounting, ahead of the rear axle. The frame was a combination of tubes and the Mustang had a fully independent suspension. The engine developed 109 horsepower at 6,400 rpm, making it ideal to compete with cars like the MGA, Alfa Romeo Giulietta Spyder, Porsche 1600, Sunbeam Alpine, and Triumph TR4. *Ford Historical Collection*

at distances of up to 1-1/2 miles. Maneuverable in all directions, the car had a removable fiberglass body mounted on a radio-controlled chassis designed for rapid interchangeability of body shells. The headlights retracted under two doors set into the nose of the car.

1960 Quicksilver

Joe Oros described a special car that was developed in the advanced section, which was also a part of the Ford Studio. It was called "Quicksilver." George Walker called it "Snowflake." It was two years ahead of its time because a completely new understructure was needed to make it work. The floors were lowered, and the big tunnel was eliminated. The overall car was lowered. When Henry Ford II saw the car, he was so enthused about it and George Walker was also so enthused that it was decided to make the 1960 Ford "X" car into the actual production car, and carry over 1959 frames and engineering for time and cost reasons.

1961 Gyron

The two-wheeled Gyron was a 3/8-scale model that ran on two wheels, but had two additional "training wheels" for when the gyro was switched off. The Gyron had automatic computer controls that would allow the driver to sit back and watch the road ahead on an infrared screen. Either of the two passengers could steer the car using dials rather than a steering wheel.

1962 Mustang I

Lee Iacocca's road to the presidency of the Ford Motor Company began with the concept that the new generation of baby boomers would be looking for a sporty car to drive. Iacocca wanted "a real show-stopper concept vehicle to knock the socks off the enthusiast press at the 1963 model introduction" in the fall of 1962. Ford didn't have any sporty cars in its lineup. What eventually became the 1964-1/2 Mustang began life as the Mustang I, a midengine two-

The 3/8 scale model Seattle-ite XXI was built for the 1962 Seattle World's Fair. It was designed for "compact nuclear propulsion devices." It also had a bubble top; gullwing doors; a jet exhaust; and six wheels, four in front and two in the rear. *Ford Historical Collection*

seat sports car. It was developed by Englishman Roy Lunn and engineer Frank Theyleg, using the German Ford Taunus 1.5-liter V-4 engine with a midship mounting, ahead of the rear axle. The frame was a combination of tubes, and the Mustang had a fully independent suspension.

Gene Bordinat, John Najjar, and Jim Sipple designed the body of the Mustang as a low roadster with a chiseled nose. It had functional side cooling scoops and a prancing horse logo. According to Ford historian Gary Witzenburg, when race driver Dan Gurney saw the designs while he was visiting the Ford design studios, he said, "That's more like it,"

West Coast custom car builders Trautman and Barnes built the aluminum body with an integral roll bar. The steering wheel and all pedals were adjustable to fit the driver, since the seats were fixed in the structurally rigid passenger compartment.

The Mustang I had a 90-inch wheelbase and was 154.3 inches long, 61 inches wide, and 39.4 inches high at the top of the roll bar. The engine developed 109 horsepower at 6,400 rpm, making it ideal to compete with such cars as the MGA, Alfa Romeo Giulietta Spyder, Porsche 1600, Sunbeam Alpine, and Triumph TR4.

The Mustang I was introduced to the public on October 7, 1962, at the U.S. Grand Prix at Watkins Glen,

Palomar featured a flying bridge for rear passengers. The rear portion of the roof would roll back, like a roll-top desk, and the forward-facing rear seat would move up. *Ford Historical Collection*

Cougar 406 was designed to resemble the Mercedes-Benz 300SL. Like the Mercedes, the Cougar 406 had gullwing doors and flush sides. Built on a 102.3-inch wheelbase, the Cougar 406 was powered by a 6.6-liter V-8 engine that developed 300 horsepower. *Ford Historical Collection*

N.Y., less than five months after it was initially authorized, and later that month at Laguna Seca in California. Dan Gurney drove the car. He did a couple of demonstration laps and reached 120 miles per hour at one point. He remembered, more than 30 years later, "It was lighter and smaller than anything else around. It could have been fun. My general recollection is one of being positive. I felt like I had a positive attitude, but I didn't have time to become familiar with it. That was the first time I sat in the car and that was the end of it."

Roy Lunn presented a paper at the January 1963 SAE Automotive Engineering Congress and Exposition in Detroit, where he went into the development of "Ford's Experimental Sports Car." Lunn explained that the Mustang "was intended to incorporate advanced styling and engineering concepts, and at the same time to have competitive potential in every aspect with the established sports cars with the same engine size.

"If we were to design a sports car with low-cost potential, it was evident that the engine and transmission units would have to be derived from an existing high-volume product line," he continued. "The engine/transmission combination that was chosen was the German 12M (Cardinal) V-4 with FWD four-speed transaxle. The V-4 and transaxle unit permitted a FWD with forward engine or a rear drive with the engine located forward of the rear axle. The rear drive/midship location was chosen, which allowed the development of a cleaner, low-drag front end and offered improved weight distribution for a two-seater car."

Lunn also explained that an aluminum skin and space frame were chosen for the first prototype. The welded space frame was constructed of 1-inch diameter, .064-inch-thick round tubes of 4130 steel. The body skin was hand formed from .060-inch aluminum sheet and was designed as a semi-unitized construction with the frame. Including the seats as part of the body skin added to the overall structural strength. However, in order to provide for varying sizes of drivers, an adjustable pedal mechanism was developed. The prototype was designed with a wraparound competition windshield, but designs for road-version windshields and stowable soft tops were under consideration.

Ford's "Better Idea" was the more popular production Mustang that debuted a little more than two years later. Iacocca was quoted as saying, "All the buffs said, 'Hey what a car. It'll be the best car ever built.' But when I looked at the guys saying it—the off-beat crowd, the real buffs, I said that's sure not the car we want to build because it can't be a volume car. It's too far out."

1962 Seattle-ite XXI

This 3/8-scale model was built for the 1962 Seattle World's Fair. Like the Nucleon before it, the Seattle-ite XXI was designed for "compact nuclear propulsion devices."

It also had a bubble top; gullwing doors; a jet exhaust; and six wheels, four in front and two in the rear. This super-sleek two-seater was, according to styling chief Gene Bordinat, "an example of the kind of exploration that can lead to key breakthroughs in automotive design."

1962 Palomar

The Palomar featured a flying bridge for rear passengers. The rear portion of the roof would roll back, like a roll-top

Mustang II was a two-plus-two. It was designed to accommodate comfortably two front-seat passengers plus two more passengers in a minimal rear seat area. It had a front-mounted, 289 ci. V-8 engine with a four-throat carburetor. *Ford Historical Collection*

Companion to the Mustang II, the Allegro was described by Ford as "a car of the future that could be built today." Mimicking Mustang styling, the Allegro had a long hood with the grille extending forward of the headlights, and a compact passenger compartment that was enclosed by a fastback roof. *Ford Historical Collection*

desk, and the forward-facing rear seat would move up. A second windshield was mounted on the roof to keep the rear passengers from being buffeted by the wind.

1962 Cougar 406

This two-seater sports car was designed to resemble the Mercedes-Benz 300SL. Like the Mercedes, the Cougar 406 had gullwing doors and flush sides. Built on a 102.3-inch wheelbase, the Cougar 406 was powered by a 6.6-liter V-8 engine that developed 300 horsepower.

1963 Mustang II

This car followed the natural evolution from the Mustang I two-seater toward the eventual production Mustang, introduced on April 17, 1964. Ford advertising noted, "In auto buff lingo, Mustang II is a two-plus-two, meaning it is designed to comfortably accommodate two front-seat passengers plus two more passengers in a minimal

rear seat area. The model is capable of outstanding performance from its front-mounted, 289 cu. in. V-8 engine with a four-Venturi carburetor. The Mustang II is 186.6 inches long on a 108-inch wheelbase. Overall width is 68.2 inches, overall height 48.4 inches. The hardtop roof, a refinement of the Thunderbird roof design, is detachable."

Round instruments were deeply recessed in the padded instrument panel, although these would be replaced by Falcon-based dials in the production car.

1963 Allegro

Companion to the Mustang II, the Allegro was described by Ford as "a car of the future that could be built today." Mimicking Mustang styling, the Allegro had a long hood with the grille extending forward of the headlights. The compact passenger compartment was enclosed by a fastback roof. Inside, the Allegro combined some elements from the Mustang I with new ones. It incorporated further

Probe 1

Probe III was a preview of the German Ford Sierra that was to appear in 1982. To achieve the remarkable low coefficient of 0.22, several aerodynamic features were included, such as flush headlamps and window glass, skirted rear wheels, full wheel discs, aerodynamic rear mirrors, and a front molding that was an extension of the front body panels. *Ford Historical Collection*

Probe IV *Ford Historical Society*

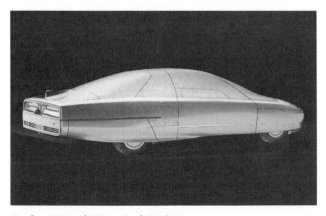

Probe V *Ford Historical Society*

advances in adjustable accelerator and brake pedals with fixed seats and retractable seat belts. Most prominent was a cantilevered-arm steering wheel with a memory unit that pivoted on the centrally mounted steering column. Button controls allowed the driver to position the wheel for the most comfort.

In its brochure, Ford called the Allegro a practical dream car that was developed jointly by stylists and engineers.

> *Its styling is daring and different, an approach in keeping with the times. Symbolizing sleekness, motion and, as its name indicates, brisk and lively performance, the Allegro is distinguished by a long hood, compact passenger compartment and a "fastback" roofline with grille wastegate in the fender area.*
>
> *The dramatic but functional interior has fixed contoured seats that are an integral part of the body structure, a feature tested in the experimental Mustang. Pedals are adjustable fore and aft by means of power switches on the steering column. The column itself is a unique cantilevered arm that can be power-adjusted fore and aft, up and down. This "idea car" incorporates many new design concepts and new features tailored to existing engine driveline and frame components.*

It is interesting to note that Ford's adjustable pedal concept took 37 years to reach production in the 2000 Ford models.

The dimensions of the Allegro were such that it could accommodate four passengers, even though the car itself was a two-seater. The wheelbase was 99 inches, overall length 169.5 inches, height 49.6 inches, and width 63.6 inches.

1965 Bertone Mustang

Built at the request of L. Scott Bailey of *Automobile Quarterly,* the Bertone Mustang 2+2 had headlights that retracted behind the outer portion of the grille. The fastback rear treatment incorporated a larger glass area than the production car. One of the requirements for the design was that it retain most of the stock body sheet-metal inner panels. Therefore, dimensions of the Bertone car were essentially identical to those of the stock car.

Splash was conceived as a corporate-refined 2+2-seater dune buggy that stretched styling bounds. Splash was built with four-wheel drive to make it as home on the ski slopes as on the beach. It also had adjustable body height to enable it to negotiate deeply rutted roads. *Ford Historical Collection*

1981 Probe III

Unveiled at the Frankfurt Motor Show, the Probe III was a preview of the German Ford Sierra that was to appear in 1982. While previous Probes were American designs, this one was a European design.

To achieve the remarkable low drag coefficient of 0.22, several aerodynamic features were included on the Probe III, such as flush headlamps and window glass, skirted rear wheels, full wheel discs, aerodynamic rear mirrors, and a front molding that was an extension of the front body panels. To further reduce turbulence, the space between the tires and the wheel arches was reduced to the minimum. The tray under the body was a flat panel, further enhancing aerodynamics. A five-piece affair, the front was what Ford called a "venturi belly pan." It was motorized and would lower at speeds in excess of 40 kilometers per hour (about 25 miles per hour) from its "safety" position where it would be protected from damage by curbs. The Probe III also had dual rear spoilers like the earlier Merkur that smoothed the airflow over the rear of the car.

The Probe III was a semi-fastback design with flush-fitting windows that had no gaps between the glass and the pillars. The flat wheel covers had small inlet holes to admit cooling air to the brakes. Even the door mirror was redesigned for aerodynamics, with a duct that prevented air turbulence. The design produced a mirror that had a 50 percent lower drag coefficient than conventional mirrors.

The Probe III had no engine, but with its aerodynamics could use a low-powered engine to achieve excellent highway speeds and fuel economy. The critical dimensions included a wheelbase of 101.9 inches, overall length of 182.5 inches, width of 68.5 inches, and height of 60 inches.

1989 Splash

Three of the dream cars Ford Motor Company showed at the 1989 Detroit Auto Show were fairly conservative by dream car standards. The fourth—the Ford Splash—was not. Conceived as a corporate-refined 2+2–seater dune buggy, the Splash stretched styling

Ghia's design studio in Turin, Italy, designed the roadster Zig to accept the engine and transmission from the Fiesta (Ford's Korean-built minicar). Alternate power sources were also possible. The forward position of the Zig and the steep slant of the windshield were similar to those of a racing motorcycle. *Ford Historical Collection*

bounds. This car was designed at the Center for Creative Studies. The charter Jack Telnack—Ford's vice president for design—gave the students was to design a vehicle that a customer could use throughout the year, not just on summer weekends.

Therefore, the Splash was built with four-wheel drive to make it as at home on the ski slopes as on the beach. It also had adjustable body height to enable it to negotiate deeply rutted roads.

The Splash had an extravagant design and a wedge shape that was defined by the front and rear fenders. A bubble roof enclosed the passengers. Inside, the two-tone gray and blue fluorescent design had magenta accents. The instruments were arrayed in a pod in front of the driver with

Painted in solid white with high-visibility color graphics to differentiate it from Zig and to reflect its multipurpose leisure theme, Zag shared common lower body sides and door panels with Zig, as well as many basic interior design features. Zag had removable rear seats, and the front passenger seat could slide forward to increase the carrying capacity. *Ford Historical Collection*

all switches wrapped around the instrument panel. The seats used material found in skin-diving wet suits. Even the tire tread was unique, giving the Splash a youthful air.

Dimensionally, the Splash was 142.9 inches long and 70.1 inches wide.

1991 Ghia Zig

Ghia's design studio in Turin, Italy, designed two cars for Ford for 1991: the roadster Zig and the coupe Zag. The Zig, according to Ford, offered "a logical alternative to conventional types of transport by reducing package size to a minimum." It was Ford's idea that other types of vehicles could be built off the same basic platform.

The Zig was designed to accept the engine and transmission from the Fiesta (Ford's Korean-built minicar). Alternate power sources were also possible.

The forward position of the Zig and the steep slant of the windshield were similar to those of a racing motorcycle. The windshield was incorporated into the front hood and lifted as a unit for easy access to the engine. A fully functional fiber-optic lighting system, featuring a row of miniaturized lenses, was molded into a slot above the bumper.

Inside, rally-type seats with three-point inertia-reel harness positioned the driver and passenger securely. The two seats were trimmed in a bright blue stretch fabric with high-contrast color inserts. A removable CD player and large door bins were additional features. Behind the seats, a

roller-type door gave access to the luggage space, which was protected by a plexiglass cover and a package tray.

"Our designers felt that it was important to develop a pair of colors in order to reinforce the relationship between [Zig and Zag]," said Filippo Sapino, managing director of Ghia. "The theme of black and white was strongly favored for the exterior body colors. Zig is painted in black mica."

1991 Ghia Zag

Painted in solid white with high-visibility color graphics to differentiate it from the Zig and to reflect its multipurpose leisure theme, the Zag shared common lower body sides and door panels with the Zig, as well as many basic interior design features. Because the Zag was aimed at people who needed a practical and versatile vehicle for the pursuit of varied activities, it had removable rear seats. The front passenger seat could slide forward to increase the carrying capacity. The seats were trimmed in a durable nylon fabric, with exposed tubes of the seat structure brightly colored for high contrast.

The microsize ultralight Zag was equipped with a Fiesta engine when it made its world debut at the 1990 Geneva International Auto Show. It was later fitted with an experimental two-stroke Orbital engine. This extremely compact engine produced about 80 horsepower and gave the Zag an excellent horsepower-to-weight ratio.

The Zag was built on an 85-inch wheelbase and was equipped with full-size alloy wheels fitted with low-profile tires. The compact overall dimensions were achieved using short front and rear overhangs.

1991 Explorer Desk Drive

Described as "the ideal vehicle for people who have to get the job done on the road," the Explorer Desk Drive was a modified sport utility vehicle that was fully equipped with state-of-the-art office and communications products as well

Contour was a New Wave global luxury sedan with contemporary proportions. It had an expanded interior compartment and reduced overall size. Contour was designed around an extruded aluminum space frame that demonstrated new construction techniques that allowed for light weight, high strength, and low investment body structures. *Ford Historical Collection*

Ford's Mustang Mach III dream car celebrated the 30th anniversary of the original (production) Mustang. Mach III brought up to date all the styling cues of the original Mustang in a much sleeker form. For example, there was the prancing pony in the grille opening, but that opening was smaller and had swooping "cat's eye" headlights on either side of it. *Ford Historical Collection*

as convenience features such as a premium sound system, television, microwave oven, refrigerator, and coffee maker. "It's an executive office on wheels," said Andrew Johnson, Ford truck design director.

The Explorer Desk Drive was powered by the standard 4.0-liter V-6 engine that powered the production car. The roof was raised about 4 inches to facilitate the required office space. Special wheels and tires, as well as a light bar with running bar that was integral with the roof, were also installed.

Inside there was much more. The Desk Drive had a computer with a 7-inch screen capable of displaying television-quality messages and advertisements through a VCR and a printer, a cellular telephone, and a fax machine. There was also a satellite antenna on the roof with an inside receiver, a dash-panel navigation system with a lighted display of the metro streets and roads network, a voice-actuated memo pad, a computer-drafting light pencil, an active noise cancellation system, and a system to secure all of the electronic equipment.

1991 Contour

Ford set out to create a New Wave global luxury sedan with contemporary proportions when it began design of the Contour, according to Jack Telnack, vice president of design. To reach this goal the designers expanded the interior compartment and reduced the overall size of the vehicle.

One way to improve fuel economy was through the use of an experimental compact "T-Drive" engine and transmission configuration that allowed designers to reduce the size of the engine compartment, reduce overall length, and still increase passenger space. This powertrain layout used a transversely mounted engine and longitudinal transmission and enabled the vehicle to be configured in front-wheel drive, rear-wheel drive, or all-wheel-drive configurations.

The Contour was designed around an extruded aluminum space frame that demonstrated new construction techniques that allowed for light weight, high strength, and low investment body structures.

Highly efficient, "high intensity discharge metal vapor" arc lamps provided power to fiber-optic headlamps, and a next-generation halogen lamp provided power to the taillamps. The taillamps were integrated within the movable aerodynamic spoilers that seemed to float above the sheet-metal surface. Unique, slender headlamps with both high and low beams were located behind acrylic lenses.

The front suspension consisted of a composite transverse-mounted single leaf spring to provide the functions of suspension spring, upper suspension arm, and stabilizer bar. The rear suspension was similar to the front and was designed as a module for ease of assembly.

The driver-oriented interior was ergonomically expressed through a movable interlock of pedals, instrument panel, and controls. The steering column could be adjusted relative to the front seat for maximum driving comfort. The instrument cluster had a gas discharge cold cathode source that emitted a diffused white light, reducing eyestrain and glare. A dark lens concealed the normally visible hardware.

1995 Mustang Mach III

To celebrate the 30th anniversary of the original (production) Mustang, Ford brought out the Mach III concept car. The Mach III brought up to date all the styling cues of the original Mustang in a much sleeker form. For example, there was the prancing pony in the grille opening, but that opening was smaller and had swooping "cat's eye" headlights on either side of it. The faux side scoops of the original were replaced with true huge scoops that ducted air to the rear disc brakes.

SHO-Star combined the Taurus SHO engine with a modified Windstar minivan. The 3.0-liter SHO engine in the SHO-Star was more powerful (220 horsepower) than in the Taurus, thanks to a special low-restriction exhaust system. The entire van was lowered and had special front and rear bumper facings, special creamy-yellow pearlescent paint, integrated lower bodyside cladding and wheel-lip moldings, blacked-out B-pillars, and chrome-plated dual exhausts. *Ford Historical Collection*

Ford's Triton dream truck was at the 1996 North American International Auto Show in Detroit. Carbon fiber was used for the grille, hood scoops, taillight bezels, and the aerodynamic tonneau that covered the bed. The tonneau had three hatches, two that opened at the center located in front and a third in the rear. *Ford Historical Collection*

"Obviously we can't bring back the 1965 Mustang," said Fritz Mayhew, chief design executive—North American Design, "but the Mach III brings back the spirit of the 1965 Mustang with styling and technology for the 1990s and beyond."

The Mach III was an open-air roadster with carbon-fiber body panels, a short, low windshield, wraparound rear bumper, and 19-inch chrome wheels. Painted in a bright fluorescent red, the paint flowed into the interior, which had seating for two. The gauges were large, round, white dials positioned for the driver's convenience. The three-spoke, wood-rimmed steering wheel was reminiscent of the Mustang's heritage. Racing-type leather seats provided for maximum comfort and lateral support.

Under the hood was a supercharged 4.6-liter 32-valve V-8 engine rated at 450 horsepower. The engine used a "cold pack" intercooler and had dual exhausts. Zero-to-60-miles-per-hour times were estimated at less than 4.5 seconds using the six-speed manual transmission. The Mach III also used a flexible fuel system, meaning it could run on gasoline, M85, or any combination of the two fuels. Sensors in the fuel line gauged how much methanol was in the fuel supply.

Four-wheel disc brakes with ABS stopped this pony. The front brakes were 13 inches in diameter, while the rear brakes were 12 inches in diameter. Brakes were "anti fade," which gave the car tremendous stopping power even after repeated hard braking actions.

The critical dimensions were a wheelbase of 101.3 inches, overall length of 188.6 inches, width of 76.6 inches, and height of 46.3 inches.

1995 SHO-Star

This vehicle, introduced at the Detroit Auto Show, combined the Taurus SHO engine with a modified Windstar minivan. However, the 3.0-liter SHO engine in the SHO-Star was more powerful (220 horsepower) than the engine in the Taurus, thanks to a special low-restriction exhaust system. This engine drove the front wheels through a five-speed manual transmission.

The suspension was also modified, and included 17-inch wheels with Michelin XGT-Z tires. The entire van was lowered and had special front and rear bumper facings, special creamy-yellow pearlescent paint, integrated lower bodyside cladding and wheel-lip moldings, blacked-out B-pillars, and chrome-plated dual exhausts. The headlights were high-intensity discharge projection-type, with fog lamps illuminated by fiber-optic cable from a high-intensity infrared light source. The other lighting on the SHO-Star was also high tech, using light-emitting diodes, halogen sources, and a gas-discharge CHMSL.

Inside, the SHO-Star had seating for seven, with two buckets in front, two in the second bank, and three "simulated buckets" on the rear bench.

1995 Triton

As Ford was designing its next-generation F-150 pickup truck, it debuted the Triton concept truck at the 1996 North American International Auto Show in Detroit. The Triton was longer, taller, and wider than the generation F-150. It had a longer wheelbase for better handling, and a new 4.6-liter V-8 engine that delivered more power more efficiently than the older 5.0-liter V-8. With 18-inch wheels at all four corners, the Triton also had disc brakes behind them.

Carbon fiber was used for the grille, hood scoops, taillight bezels, and the aerodynamic tonneau that covered the bed. The tonneau had three hatches, two that opened at the center located in front and a third in the rear.

The lights were by Ford and Sylvania in a new "cold bulb" gas-discharge technology. These included the headlights, CHMSL, back-up lights, cargo lights, and turn indicators.

Ford's GT90 small sports car drew on Ford's GT40 racing heritage. It was unlike anything else the automaker was exhibiting that year. The 6.0-liter V-12 had four turbochargers, which helped boost output to 720 horsepower. Top speed was a theoretical 235 miles per hour. The carbon fiber body showcased Ford's "New Edge" design philosophy with sharp edges and crisp lines. *Mike Mueller*

1996 GT90

Ford customarily introduces its show cars for the Detroit Auto Show at its media Christmas party held in December, about one month before the show. The automotive press was shocked when A. J. Foyt drove the GT90 out from behind a curtain in 1995. This small sports car, obviously drawing on Ford's GT40 racing heritage, was beautiful and unlike anything else the automaker was exhibiting that year.

For example, the 6.0-liter V-12 had four turbochargers, which helped boost output to 720 horsepower. The engine itself was built up of two V-8 engines from the Lincoln Mark III. The engines had two cylinders removed from the front and rear, respectively, and then were welded together and shared a common crankshaft. Foyt, who had won the Le Mans 24-hour race at the wheel of a Ford Mark II, said he'd be ready to un-retire if Ford seriously wanted to race the car. The top speed was a theoretical 235 miles per hour.

The engine was located ahead of the rear axle in a honeycomb aluminum monocoque chassis. The body was a carbon-fiber affair that showcased Ford's "New Edge" design philosophy with sharp edges and crisp lines. Tom Scott, director of advanced design, said he let the body's surfaces be dictated by the airflow that turned and rolled as the air pattern advanced.

The GT90 was also a "triangular" body in that it had repeated triangular shapes all over it. The taillamps, four clustered exhaust pipes, air intakes, and interior all had triangular shapes.

For technology, the rear C-pillar blind spot had an infrared beam that would warn the driver of nearby vehicles.

1996 Synergy 2010

A diesel/electric hybrid that had a flywheel in the nose to store energy, the Synergy 2010 was Ford's effort at developing a car that could average 80 miles per gallon. Part of that fuel efficiency was contributed by an extremely low coefficient of drag of .20 and a low weight of 2,205 pounds. Both were achieved by an aluminum monocoque body with unique front fenders that acted as manifolds, sweeping back from the front bumper area toward the car's body. These manifolds provided cooling air, but they also housed television cameras that replaced traditional mirrors.

In the rear was a 1.0-liter direct-injection diesel motor that served both as a propulsion source and to generate electricity for motors attached to each wheel.

Instruments were voice-actuated, with a heads-up display mounted on the steering column.

Synergy 2010 was a diesel/electric hybrid that had a flywheel in the nose to store energy. It was Ford's effort at developing a car that could average 80 mpg. The aluminum monocoque body had unique front fenders that acted as manifolds sweeping back from the front bumper area toward the car's body. *Ford Historical Collection*

General Motors

General Motors Corp. was, of course, behind all dream car development credited to the individual brands. Earlier there were separate studios, but at the present time the studios are located in fairly close proximity.

But GM does take credit for four unique vehicles: three turbine-powered Firebirds and the electric Impact. The Firebirds were visually exciting and had progressively more-developed engines. Turbine technology never made it to production, but it wasn't the fault of GM's design staffs.

As for the Impact, it may or not be a production car. The infrastructure still isn't in place in 2000 for serious electric car production, although the vehicles are useful for short runs in controlled circumstances. But this is a design study, and the Impact had an impact on modern car design.

GM Design

In the 1938 publication "Modes and Motors," put out by the Styling Section of General Motors, the following defined the role of the designer in the development of the automobile:

"The job of the designer is to combine the mechanical requirements with the human requirements—to bring together the science of the engineer and the skill of the artist in order that the automobile might be as beautiful as it is useful.

"Always there is a race between our ideals of what a thing should be like and our ability to make it that way. Design frequently waits upon technological advancement before the product can be made as the artist pictures it in his mind—upon new materials, and upon mechanical improvements in the car itself. Finally, every improvement

in design must always be measured in the terms of the cost of this benefit to the user."

Many of the vehicles that came out of GM during the "glory years" were pure fantasy, such as the Firebirds described below. Such is not necessarily the case at GM, Ford, or Chrysler today. Wayne Cherry, vice president of design at GM, described it this way:

> [The dream cars of today] definitely are coming right out of the work we're doing for the product portfolio. I think some of the vehicles . . . with Harley Earl,—depending on whether you're referring to Firebirds or LeSabres—Firebirds were showing technology and the world of the future. I think vehicles like the Y-Job and the LeSabre were showing more where the design, generically, would be going in automobiles. They were very influential in a lot of the production vehicles GM was doing at that period of time.
>
> Today, what you're seeing is a total company working together holistically, whether it's engineering or planning or design or R&D, in developing an innovative product portfolio. Our objective is to become the industry leader in product innovation. These [modern dream cars] have the engineering and the packaging and the design as total holistic vehicles that are under evaluation for our product planning.

Firebird I showed Harley Earl's fascination with aero themes. The car incorporated a needle nose from a jet fighter, a bubble cockpit, delta wings, and a tail fin. The Firebird I body was constructed of plastic reinforced with fiberglass. The turbine engine was located in the rear. *John Heilig*

The second generation Firebird took gas turbine technology, as well as design, to the next level. Where Firebird I had room for only a driver, there was seating for four in Firebird II. The car also included such innovations as electric windows, electric transmission, and air conditioning. Firebird II also demonstrated the first use of four-wheel disc brakes, a fully independent four-wheel suspension, and an electronic guidance system for use on "highways of the future." *John Heilig*

1954 Firebird I

A creation of Harley Earl, the Firebird I shows Earl's fascination with aero themes. The car incorporates a needle nose from a jet fighter, a bubble cockpit, delta wings, and a tail fin. The Firebird I body was constructed of plastic reinforced with fiberglass. The 35-gallon fuel tank, located in the nose of the car, was also built of fiberglass-reinforced plastic. The turbine engine was located in the rear.

The first Firebird was designed as a turbine showcase, but nothing could deter Earl and his creative staff from using it as a styling showcase as well. This car debuted at the 1954 Motorama at the Waldorf-Astoria Hotel in New York. Its genesis was a Douglas F4D Skyray jet plane. Earl had seen photos of the delta-winged fighter and showed them to Bob McLean for inspiration. According to Michael Lamm

Seating dropped two positions for Firebird III, which first saw the light of day in 1958. The two passengers rode under individual plexiglass bubbles. GM replaced the traditional steering wheel, brake pedal, and accelerator with an all-in-one joystick, and the instrument panel was straight off an airplane. *John Heilig*

in *Collectible Automobile*, "McLean's job was basically to translate the Skyray into a fiberglass-bodied Motorama showstopper: a single-seater, nominally a 'sports car,' with the driver shoved forward under a Plexiglas bubble and a turbine engine behind."

This wasn't the world's first attempt at a turbine car. Chrysler, of course, was working on its own turbine car that would hit the roads at the hands of drivers selected by lottery. And Britain's Rover had set speed records with its turbine car in Europe. Rover, in combination with BRM, would design a turbine race car and enter it at Le Mans in 1963, finishing in eighth place.

GM's Firebird used a GM "Whirlfire" GT-302 turbine engine that developed around 400 horsepower. Originally designed for truck use, it gulped gas, with fuel economy only around 5 miles per gallon. The good news was that a turbine would burn almost anything.

Wind tunnel tests showed that the Firebird could achieve more than 200 miles per hour in a speed test. Three-time Indianapolis 500 winner Mauri Rose was hired to drive the car at the GM test track near Mesa, Arizona. Charles L. McCuen, head of turbine research, decided to shake the car down at the Milford, Michigan, test track first.

Lamm reports that McCuen was fooled by the car's acceleration. When the car reached the far high-speed turn at Milford, it was going too fast. McCuen went under the guardrail and the car rolled over, totaling the body. The headrest built into the seat saved McCuen's life.

Fortunately, the female plaster body molds were still in existence and a new fiberglass body was built in time for the Motorama. Mauri Rose never drove it, though.

The Firebird I was 223 inches long overall on a 100-inch wheelbase. The height was 41 inches at the top of the bubble and 55 inches at the top of the tail fin. It weighed 2,440 pounds. Designed primarily for show and straight-line use, the four-wheel independent suspension used a deDion tube in the rear and coil springs between the upper and lower A-arms in front. It had four-wheel 11-inch Alfin brake drums.

The Firebird I design was chosen to top the trophy for the winner of the NASCAR Daytona 500, an award that is still presented.

1956 Firebird II

The second-generation Firebird took gas turbine technology, as well as design, to the next level. Whereas the

Firebird I had an exhaust temperature of 1,250°F, the regenerative gas turbine engine on the Firebird II operated almost 1,000 degrees cooler. The Firebird II also had increased seating capacity. Where the Firebird I only had room for a driver, there was seating for four in the Firebird II. The car also included such innovations as electric windows, electric transmission, and air conditioning. The Firebird II demonstrated the first use of four-wheel disc brakes, a fully independent four-wheel suspension, and an electronic guidance system for use on "highways of the future."

Earl and turbine engine engineer Bill Turunen began work on the second in the series in late 1954 for the 1956 Motorama. The engine was a GT-304, with two rotating heat exchangers that recycled the combustion energy, making the engine more fuel efficient and responsive. The maximum horsepower was down to 200, though.

McLean's studio was again asked to design the car, with the charter to make it a "Family Sedan of the Future." The result was a four-seater, again with a bubble top. Earl wanted titanium body skins, a Plexiglas bubble with aircraft-style instruments, and an aircraft-style steering wheel. The bubble opened with the then-popular gull-wing doors.

Titanium, however, was difficult to beat into panels. Eventually, the body panels were stamped out of red-hot titanium over Kirsite dies. To eliminate welds, an epoxy resin joined the panels. A second fiberglass-bodied car was built.

The Firebird II also showcased GM's new air-oil suspension. Four interconnected hydropneumatic canisters replaced the springs, much like Citroen's. An electric pump and accumulator forced oil into the canisters at pressures determined by sensors at each of the four wheels.

The Firebird II was significantly larger than its predecessor, being 235 inches long on a 120-inch wheelbase. With the lower horsepower, there was also greater weight, as the Firebird II weighed 5,300 pounds. The front and rear suspensions were independent again, with the rear now employing swing axles.

While Lamm calls the titanium Firebird II a "pushmobile," the fiberglass one definitely ran. Two GM engineers drove the car from Detroit to Atlanta and back and had no mechanical problems. Starting it up created a sound not unlike a large vacuum cleaner, and it would be interesting to see the car stretch its legs on the highway again.

1959 Firebird III

The seating dropped two positions for the Firebird III, which first saw the light of day in 1958. The two passengers rode under individual plexiglass bubbles that must have made conversation difficult. GM also replaced the traditional steering wheel, brake pedal, and accelerator with an all-in-one joystick, and the instrument panel was straight off an airplane. The joystick would permit the driver to accelerate, brake, and steer. Reverse required a 20-degree left or right twist of the handle; park required an 80-degree twist.

The Firebird III's "missile-like" styling demonstrated a tapered nose and *seven* fins. The lower fins, or "skegs," were the only Firebird III feature to make it to production cars. These would appear on the 1961 Cadillac as those cars moved away from the outrageous high fins of 1959. McLean was moving into management, and ceded design of the Firebird III to Norm James and Stefan Habsburg, which is another reason the Firebird III shifts in design from the first two. James and Habsburg were directed by Earl through McLean to follow the 1956 Pontiac Club de Mer show car and extend those themes; this resulted in the flatter tapering nose that ended in a wide low grille.

The last Firebird was the biggest. At 248 inches long overall, it rode on a 119-inch wheelbase, was 81 inches wide, and 57 inches tall at the top of the dorsal fin. The fiberglass Firebird III weighed 5,275 pounds.

The Firebird III used yet another GM turbine for power, this one tagged GT-305. It was smaller and more fuel efficient than GT-304, offering as much as 20 miles per gallon. But turbine research was slowly dying. This engine was rated at 225 horsepower at 24,000 rpm.

Former Cadillac studio head David Holls said that the Firebird III was important because it broke GM's old rules of surface development. Prior to that time, all GM cars included Earl's highlight lines in the designs. The Firebird III is almost chrome-free, which was radical for 1959.

1990 Impact

This vehicle had a profound influence on a semi-regular production car that was distributed under the GM nameplate. The 1990 Impact resulted in the 1996 EV1 electric vehicle that had limited, but regular, production.

The Impact had an extremely low coefficient of drag—0.19—to compensate for the low power of the electric motors and to aid in range. With no tailpipes or undercarriage mechanicals, the underbody could be relatively flat, which aided in the low Coefficient of drag.

The Impact was relatively light for a battery-powered car at 2,200 pounds, 900 of which were the 32 10-volt lead-acid batteries. Two three-phase AC electric motors supplied the power after the DC power of the batteries passed through a converter. Regenerative braking recharged the batteries whenever the driver applied the brakes or slowed down.

The car was a two-seater, designed for around-town driving. The claimed top speed was 100 miles per hour, with a 0-60 acceleration time of eight seconds.

CHAPTER 8

Jeep

There have only been a few Jeep dream cars and all have been true to the nature of the vehicle. Jeep dream cars didn't even exist until the 1991 Wagoneer, which is hard to differentiate from the production Wagoneer.

Some Jeeps have pushed the envelope of design, but it's a small envelope. Chrysler Corporation is not going to mess with one of its most successful products, and while the corporation may tweak the design of Jeeps, it probably won't get too carried away. It's safer to exercise design talents on a Dodge or Chrysler.

1991 Wagoneer

Recalling a name from Jeep's storied past, Wagoneer met the challenge of designing a vehicle that retained traditional Jeep styling cues and had the attributes and innovative features that made Jeep a household name. Unlike the boxy wartime Jeeps, the Wagoneer had long, fluid lines that swept back from the low-slung hood. Along with flush-mounted glass, the Wagoneer had a shape that slipped effortlessly through the wind. The low, sculpted front end hinted at the powerful 220-horsepower 5.2-liter V-8 engine lurking under the hood. A built-in step dropped out of each doorsill to ease entry and egress. An innovative flush-mounted roof rack could pop up to accommodate extra luggage. The tailgate would drop down to reveal removable stadium seats for tailgating, picnics, or fishing.

Inside were leather seats that could be converted into either two bench seats or six swivel captain's chairs. The Wagoneer's interior also included wood accents and a movable entertainment center.

1997 Dakar

Based on the Jeep Wrangler, the Dakar was unveiled at the 1997 North American International Auto Show in Detroit. The Dakar was unusual in that it had four doors, accomplished by stretching the Wrangler wheelbase to 108.5 inches, almost 15 inches more than the standard Wrangler.

The Dakar was also given a new windshield, side glass, and an all-new steel roof. The roof also offered a variety of features, including a full-length built-in tubular rack, as well as a manual canvas sliding sunroof, front-mounted rally lamps, spare tire storage, and strategically placed handrails that ran the length of the D-pillar. Other multipurpose features included a folding shovel integrated into the front fender, jerry cans built into the rear tailgate, and an "adventure module" designed to fit inside of the rear door that included a night vision scope, binoculars, flashlight, and compass.

Obviously a Jeep, the Dakar was 166.5 inches long, 72.0 inches wide, and 75.0 inches tall. The 15-inch cast-aluminum wheels wore 31x10.5 Goodyear Wrangler ST tires. The 4.0-liter V-6 engine was connected to a four-speed automatic transmission.

Wagoneer met the challenge of designing a vehicle that retained traditional Jeep styling cues and had the attributes and innovative features that made Jeep a household name. Wagoneer had long, fluid lines that swept back from the low-slung hood. A built-in step dropped out of each door sill to ease entry and egress. Daimler Chrysler Historical Collection

Based on the Jeep Wrangler, Dakar was unusual in that it had four doors, accomplished by stretching the Wrangler wheelbase. Dakar was also given a new windshield, side glass, and an all-new steel roof, which offered a variety of features, including a full-length built-in tubular roof rack. *Daimler Chrysler Historical Collection*

1997 Icon

The Icon was another creative exploration for a next-generation Jeep Wrangler, according to John E. Herlitz, Chrysler Corporation's vice president of product design. The Icon had a compact muscular look that was achieved by increasing the size of its bumpers, tires, and wheel arches. "We widened Wrangler's track, reduced its length by five inches, its overhang by two inches, and increased wheel travel from eight to ten inches," said Trevor Creed, Chrysler's design director.

Traditional Wrangler styling cues, such as long dash-to-axle proportions, classic grille, exposed hinges, folding windshield, and roll cage were redefined and updated for the new millennium. The Icon was painted Steel Blue Metallic. The interior was deliberately simple and rugged with exposed aluminum fittings and painted steel.

1998 Jeepster

Once again, a Jeep dream car took its name from a previous production Jeep model. Looking like a cross between a dune buggy and a Jeep, the 1998 Jeepster concept vehicle was defined by Jeep as "a V-8 powered sports car that can cover the Rubicon Trail, the granddaddy of off-road excursions."

"This project began as a Jeep studio designer initiative to create a crossover vehicle," said Mike Moore, Chrysler's chief designer for the interior and exterior of Jeep products. "It was a 'what if' exercise. What if you could have the

Icon was an exploration for a next-generation Jeep Wrangler. It had a compact muscular look that was achieved by increasing the size of its bumpers, tires, and wheel arches. Traditional Wrangler styling cues, such as long dash-to-axle proportions, classic grille, exposed hinges, folding windshield, and roll cage were redefined and updated for the new millennium. *Daimler Chrysler Historical Collection*

power and excitement of a sports car coupled with the capability and rugged go-anywhere nature of a Jeep Wrangler?"

The Jeepster had an electronic four-wheel independent adjustable suspension that could raise or lower the vehicle 4 inches to negotiate rugged off-road conditions and adjust the attitude for a more aerodynamic on-road ride. On-road, the Jeepster had a ground clearance of 5-3/4 inches, which improved ride and handling by lowering the center of gravity and better managing the air flow. Off-road, the vehicle could be adjusted to a 9-3/4-inch ground clearance, necessary for serious rock climbing. In addition, the Jeepster had short overhangs, a four-speed Quadra-Trac II transmission, and an aluminum skid plate integrated in the side sill.

The two-plus-two-seater was equipped with a 4.7-liter SOHC 16-valve V-8 engine that developed an estimated 275 horsepower. The transmission was a four-speed automatic with a viscous coupled full-time transfer case and a Dana 44 final drive front and rear.

The body was painted an intense red with contrasting deep blue fender flares and side panels. The traditional seven-slot Jeep grille was flanked by uniquely detailed head-lamps, placed high on the steeply raked grille for lighting efficiency. The front of the hood was lowered for maximum visibility. Inside, the instrument panel had a military radio look that retained images of past Jeep military products. The heater controls were arranged concentrically. The Jeepster even included a navigation system that was a reconfigurable colored flat screen technology display, which included a GPS system, an altimeter, grade and roll indicator, and an exterior temperature sensor. The cognac-colored seats were made of weather-resistant leather similar to hiking boots. The tires were Goodyear 255/55R19 Extended Mobility Tires that were capable of maintaining their shape on- and off-road, even after a flat, at speeds up to 55 miles per hour for 50 miles.

1999 Commander

Shown at the 1999 Detroit International Auto Show, the Jeep Commander not only explored the challenge of an aerodynamic Jeep, it also explored alternative forms of propulsion. Jeep engineers said they believed the Commander was the only four-wheel-drive vehicle that ran

Looking like a Jeep dune buggy, the Jeepster concept vehicle was defined by Jeep as "a V-8 powered sports car that can cover the Rubicon Trail, the granddaddy of off-road excursions." Jeepster had an electronic four-wheel independent adjustable suspension that could raise or lower the vehicle four inches to negotiate rugged off-road conditions and adjust the attitude for a more aerodynamic on-road ride. *John Heilig*

on electric power. Under the hood were two EPIC minivan electric motors, one for each axle, which provided full-time four-wheel drive. Electricity was to be generated in a fuel cell by combining hydrogen and oxygen in an electrochemical reaction, but as in any true dream car, the fuel cell was not operative when the car was introduced. Chrysler said it hoped to have a working fuel cell by the end of 1999.

With a 2,100-pound fuel cell generator under the hood, body weight could become astronomic. Therefore, the designers chose to create an aerodynamic body con-

structed of injected molded plastic. The concept was built in carbon fiber to simulate the weight savings that might be achieved with plastic. Plastic technology can save as much as 50 percent of body weight, 10 to 50 percent in manufacturing costs, and is nearly 100 percent recyclable. With a final weight of 5,000 pounds, the Commander was comparable to full-size sport utilities.

"The Commander is a sophisticated, upscale sport utility vehicle," said Trevor Creed. "But from any angle, no one could mistake it for anything but a Jeep."

Exterior designer Steve Won said, "Bauhaus design philosophy led me to the very clean, precise, and mechanical appearance. It still has true Jeep character, down to the traditional seven-slot grille, but it is also ultra-modern and sophisticated."

Won added that he felt the Commander had a machined, high-tech feel. "One of the details to reinforce that image was to recreate a jet engine's intake and exhaust appearance within the headlamps and taillights."

As with any Jeep, functionality was important in the design. For example, the tow hitch cover folded down and doubled as a step for ease in reaching the roof. Sideview mirrors had wipers and 180-degree convex mirrors to eliminate blind spots.

Inside, the Commander had a space in the center console to hold a small laptop computer that could provide GPS data and Internet access for real-time weather, traffic, and directions, as well as phone, e-mail, and vehicle diagnostic information. The laptop was connected to a liquid crystal display. Embedded in the steering column was a small microphone to accept voice commands that were translated into data. There was even a small camera located within the instrument panel to take a picture of the person who steals the car, if someone were to be so rash.

The Jeep Commander was only 186 inches long, but it was wider than normal vehicles at 80 inches and was 69.4 inches high. Still, the doorsills were 2 inches lower than a 1999 Grand Cherokee. The extra width permitted three individual bucket seats in the rear and an extra-wide console in front.

For color, Chrysler designers chose a silver exterior with a blue leather interior and cognac leather trim.

Jeep Commander explored the challenge of creating an aerodynamic Jeep that used alternative forms of propulsion. Jeep engineers said they believed the Commander was the only four-wheel drive vehicle than ran on electric power. Under the hood were two EPIC minivan electric motors, one for each axle, that provided full-time four-wheel drive. *Daimler Chrysler Historical Collection*

CHAPTER 9

Lincoln and Mercury

Lincoln's first dream car was the exotic XL500. Its most recent is the Blackwood, a pseudo-production vehicle that is a cross between the Navigator sport utility and a pickup truck.

All luxury car manufacturers at the end of the century are anxious to redefine their product line with trucks and sport utilities. Lincoln is no different, and if the Blackwood does enter production, it will mark a complete redefinition of the brand.

Lincoln
1953 XL-500

With a heat-resistant bubble roof and a chrome strip across the top that acted as a transverse rollbar, the XL-500 had features that were copied by the 1955 Ford Crown Victoria. The push-button transmission and the glass roof were *not* among the copied features. In order to accommodate the low fender line, the XL-500 employed an arch over the wheels. This connected to the rear of the fenders with small fins. The exterior styling included front bumpers that curved around the front fenders without a break and continued to the rear of the car. The front air scoop was matched in the rear.

Among the unique features were "blisters" over the rear tires that allowed for extra wheel movement while still retaining a low fender line. The car was constructed of scarlet fiberglass.

The XL-500 was based on the 1953 Lincoln, with, as *Motor Trend* put it, "a more powerful version of the current engine." It was 216.25 inches long, 57 inches tall, and 81.5 inches wide. This was a big car.

The interior features included white leather upholstery with red trim. Bucket seats were up front with a bench in the rear. There was a telephone at the driver's elbow with an automatic antenna at the top of the windshield. It also had an electric calendar if you happened to forget the date. Switches located on the console between the front seats operated a voice recorder, could raise the trunk or hood, or jack up the car. The automatic transmission was operated by push buttons located in the steering wheel hub. The horn was operated by pushing a pedal. The console extended to the rear and had air conditioning and heater outlets for the two rear passengers.

Instruments were located at the base of the windshield, with a group of warning lights located at the top of the windshield. The instrument location was at the dash end of a hood scoop.

1955 Futura

The Lincoln Futura was one of those cars that wouldn't go away. After a career as (some say) the most successful Lincoln concept car ever built, it went on to star in a couple of movies and then became the Batmobile of the television series. So if the success of a concept car is judged by its lifetime, then the Futura may well have been one of the most successful.

The Lincoln XL-500 had a heat-resistant bubble roof and a chrome strip across the top that acted as a transverse rollbar. It also had a push-button transmission, a glass roof, and arches over the wheels to accommodate the low fender line. These arches connected to the rear of the fenders with small fins. *Ford Historical Collection*

The exterior of the Lincoln Futura was highlighted by a double bubble canopy and featured tail fins. The fins would make it to production Lincolns in the late 1950s. The front featured a full-width waterfall grille and deeply hooded headlights. Hubcaps had no valve stem holes in them, and the only access to the stems was from under the car. The Futura continued its life as the Batmobile of television fame. *Ford Historical Collection*

The Futura was designed by Bill Schmidt, who was the Lincoln-Mercury Division's chief stylist from 1945 to 1955. Schmidt was responsible for not only the production Lincolns, but also the XL-500 concept car.

There's an interesting tie-in between the Futura and the Chevrolet Corvette XP-755 Shark. Schmitt and GM's Bill Mitchell vacationed together in the Bahamas during the winter of 1952. Both were impressed by the tropical sea life they saw and the way the colors of the fish shimmered under the water. When both returned to Detroit, they attempted to translate their Bahamas experience into vehicle design. While Mitchell's Shark and the cars that followed were more true to the original sharks they saw, the only fish influences on the Futura were "gills" on the deck lid of the finished car.

Schmidt had assistance from John Najjar and Martin Regitko, both of whom had worked with Schmidt under Bob Gregorie on the original 1938-39 Continental. After the design of the Futura was finished, the plans were sent to Ghia in Turin for completion of the car. It was a good choice.

The Futura's chassis was one of six that had been built by Hess and Eisenhart of Cincinnati as possible Mark II chassis. The engine was "an advanced version of Lincoln's present overhead valve V-8," according to Ford press releases, and developed 330 horsepower. It incorporated an oil bath-type air cleaner that was mounted on the side of the engine because of the car's low profile.

The exterior of the Futura was highlighted by a double bubble canopy and tail fins that would make it to production Lincolns, if only in concept. The front featured a full-width waterfall grille and deeply hooded headlights. The hubcaps had no valve stem holes and the only access to the stems was from under the car. The hood was hinged at the front. Door handles were located in nacelles at the tops of the doors. When the doors opened, the interior lights went on and the top rose.

A full-width console separated the individual bucket seats, with a telephone located behind it. All gauges were located in the hub of the steering wheel. A button on the floor activated the horn. Thumb switches on the steering wheel activated the turn signals. The hub of the wheel remained stationary even when the wheel was turned. The driver chose whichever gear he or she wanted by using push buttons located on the side of the center console. The push buttons were different sizes for different gears.

When the Futura was in motion, the interior was sealed off from the outside, with no road noise transmitting itself inside. In order to hear sounds outside the car (some of the cacophony is necessary), there was a microphone in the center of the aerial on the trunk and a speaker located on a vertical chrome panel between the seats.

The Futura was first shown at the 1955 Chicago Auto Show. It was also shown at the Detroit and New York shows that year. When not on tour, it was displayed in the Ford Rotunda. After four years, its life as a concept car was nearing its end and it was sold to MGM where it "starred" in the movie *It Started With a Kiss*, with Debbie Reynolds and Glenn Ford. From there, customizer George Barris took it to his shop, where he turned it into the Batmobile for the television series.

1989 Ghia Continental

Shown at the 1989 Detroit Auto Show, the Ghia Continental was a slightly modified version of the then-current car. Among the modifications were a large front bumper

The Ghia Continental was a slightly modified version of the then-current car. Modifications included a large front bumper with built-in fog lamps and a darkened grille. Body-colored rocker panel moldings were added to the sides. The rear deck lid was replaced by one with a movable spoiler. Ghia also lowered the suspension and added 17-inch wheels to create a sportier image for the car. *Ford Historical Collection*

The Lincoln L2K was powered by an experimental 3.4-liter, 32-valve V-8 that delivered 250 horsepower and drove the rear wheels through a four-speed automatic transmission. Sporting a traditional Lincoln grille, the L2K was a two-door, two-seater convertible—something Lincoln had never offered. Under the car were full-length aerodynamic panels, much like in a formula race car. *Ford Historical Collection*

with built-in fog lamps and a darkened grille. Rocker panel moldings in the same color as the body were added to the sides. The rear deck lid was replaced by one with a movable spoiler. Ghia also lowered the suspension and added 17-inch wheels to build a sportier image for the car.

Most of the modifications were reserved for the interior, which reflected European more than American taste. Most of the surfaces were colored off-white and finished with matte surfaces. Gray walnut inserts were added to the dash and door panels. Real walnut wood was used. The seats were upholstered in off-white leather and had a blue jacquard fabric insert.

1995 L2K

In a world that was increasingly turning to front-wheel drive, Lincoln introduced the L2K rear-wheel-drive dream car in 1995 at the North American International Auto Show in Detroit. The L2K was intended to represent a Lincoln product in the year 2000.

Designed at Lincoln's California design studio, the L2K was powered by a 3.4-liter 32-valve V-8 that delivered 250 horsepower and drove the rear wheels through a four-speed automatic transmission. Both the styling and the engine were experimental. While the L2K sported a traditional Lincoln grille, what was behind that grille was a two-door, two-seater convertible, something Lincoln had never offered. The doors of the L2K had no exterior handles. To open them you pushed a button on the key fob. A spoiler was located behind the seats that reduced wind noise when riding with the top down. Under the car were full-length aerodynamic panels, much like in a formula race car. Many observers said they saw reminders of Jaguar

forms in the L2K, which was understandable, since Ford also owned Jaguar.

Inside, the upholstery was leather and the gauges were analog. The sound system included a minidisc CD changer in the rear console between the seats. The L2K also had a sizable trunk for its class, 12 cubic feet.

1996 Sentinel

Just when the world thought that nothing new would ever come from Lincoln, Ford Motor Company's luxury car

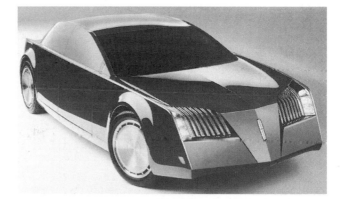

The Sentinel was based on the 1961 Lincoln Continental as well as the 1958 Facel Vega Excellence. Both featured an earlier version of what would later be called Ford's "New Edge" styling. The Sentinel rode on a wheelbase that was 22 inches longer than the Town Car's, yet the overall length was an inch shorter. Under the hood was a 6.0-liter V-12 engine, an engine that was also used in the Ford Indigo. The exterior had vertical headlights, grille slats up front, and a slight "Continental" wheel hump in the trunk. *Ford Historical Collection*

division introduced the Sentinel in 1996 at the Detroit International Auto Show. The Sentinel was based on the 1961 Lincoln Continental as well as the 1958 Facel Vega Excellence. Both featured an earlier version of what would later be called Ford's "New Edge" styling. Claude Lobo headed the design team, with contributors from all of Ford's design centers.

The Sentinel rode on a wheelbase that was 22 inches longer than the Town Car's, yet the overall length was an inch shorter. Under the hood was a 6.0-liter V-12 engine that was also used in the Ford Indigo. The exterior had vertical headlights and grille slats up front and a slight "Continental wheel" hump in the trunk.

At the Detroit show there was no interior to the Sentinel. Ghia later designed a "New Edge" interior for the car.

1999 Blackwood

The Blackwood was a four-door, four-seat sport utility vehicle/pickup truck. Lincoln called the Blackwood "the ultimate sport utility vehicle, with all the comfort of a luxury sedan and the convenience and versatility of a sport utility vehicle." Designers referred to the covered rear storage area as an extended trunk rather than a bed, and they considered the vehicle a sport utility. The trunk sides were finished in 20 square feet of Wenge wood, with a brushed-aluminum strip defining each band of wood. It was a modern twist of the "woody," which traditionally used different-colored wood strips between large wood bands.

Inside, the Blackwood was based on the Lincoln Navigator sport utility, with the addition of a GPS integrated into the floor-mounted center console. The four bucket seats were trimmed in black Connolly leather.

The name came from the use of the dark, striated Wenge wood that was used for accents inside and out, as well as the black lacquer finish on the exterior metal. The Blackwood was built on a 4x2 chassis that was lowered 3 inches for a tougher stance. Power came from a 5.4-liter

The Blackwood was a four-door, four-seat sport utility vehicle/pickup truck. Designers referred to the covered rear storage area as an extended trunk rather than a bed, and they considered the vehicle to be a sport utility. The trunk sides were finished in 20 square feet of Wenge wood, with a brushed aluminum strip defining each band. *Ford Historical Collection*

DOHC V-8 that fit it into the Class III trailer-towing group, allowing enough capacity for a boat or horse trailer.

Mercury

When you consider that Mercury began its existence as a "dream" Ford, it's surprising that there haven't been that many dream cars with Mercury labels in the 60 years of the brand's existence.

Most have been modifications of current production models, such as the Gametime Villager or the (my) Mercury. But Mercury has had a few unique cars that have earned recognition for the brand.

1962 Palomar

Introduced at the 1962 New York International Automobile Show, the Palomar station wagon had quad round headlights covered by an oval lens. It also had a unique rear treatment. The top could slide back into the rear tailgate, giving the passengers the benefits of open-air motoring. Rear-seat

The Cougar II was a two-passenger GT coupe with a fastback roof, pop-up headlights, and a fully instrumented interior. It was powered by a 260-cubic-inch high-performance V-8 engine that Ford said could be engineered to attain speeds in the 170-miles-per-hour range. Built on a 90-inch wheelbase, Cougar II was 167.8 inches long, 47.8 inches high, and 66.6 inches wide. *Ford Historical Collection*

passengers could raise their seat for a better view of the road (modern stylists would call this "theater seating") and would gain another windshield to protect them from flying bugs.

1963 Cougar II

Ford's third 1963 dream car was the Cougar II, a two-passenger GT coupe with a fastback roof, pop-up headlights, and a fully instrumented interior. The Cougar II was powered by a 260-cubic-inch high-performance V-8 engine that Ford said could be engineered to attain speeds in the 170-miles-per-hour range. Built on a 90-inch wheelbase, the Cougar II was 167.8 inches long, 47.8 inches high, and 66.6 inches wide.

The interior featured an all-black color scheme with two individually adjustable bucket seats, a console-mounted four-speed gearshift lever, and a straight-line array of instruments. The wood-and-aluminum steering wheel telescoped.

By means of a window-lift mechanism, occupants could raise or lower the curved side glass to any position. A single handle with a spring-loaded tab could be moved up or down on a ratcheted track in the door panel. When the tab was released, the window was locked in place. When the interior air pressure exceeded 15 psi, a relief panel across the rear of the passenger compartment would open automatically. This was necessary because of possible extreme pressure against the rear window at high speeds.

1965 Comet Cyclone Sportster

This was a variation of the standard 1965 Comet Cyclone that was prepared by customizer Gene Winfield for auto shows around the country. Among the interesting exterior features were air intakes that emerged from the hood that fed the engine (unspecified). Other "racing" features included a low windshield and a stylized roll bar behind the driver and passenger's head. The two-seater couldn't be started unless the seatbelts were fastened.

The steering was by two pistol-grip handles. There were no pedals on the floor, just touch pads on the floorboard for the accelerator, brake, and clutch.

1989 ONE

Many dream cars are noted for "pushing the envelope" of styling almost to the point of bursting. The Mercury ONE, introduced at the 1989 North American International Automobile Show in Detroit, was not one of these. Rather, the ONE was conservatively styled, following the lines of the then-current Mercury Sable and Ford Taurus, but in a smaller format.

Despite its strong corporate heritage, the ONE was designed in Ford's Advanced Exterior Concepts Studio under manager Darrell Behmer and director David Turner. The ONE had an enlarged greenhouse, which was separated from the lower body by a strong black belt painted on the hood and rear deck. The bases of both front and rear windows were concave.

Car Styling magazine noted: "Ford has achieved an exterior with great personality. Fundamentally, it is a healthy-type family sedan with a large cabin and a wide glass area."

Mercury's Comet Cyclone Sportster was a variation on the standard 1965 Comet Cyclone that was prepared by customizer Gene Winfield for auto shows around the country. Among the interesting exterior features were air intakes that emerged from the hood to feed the engine. Other "racing" features included a low windshield and a stylized rollbar behind the driver and passenger's head. Steering was by two pistol-grip handles. *Ford Historical Collection*

1989 Concept 50

Unlike the conservative ONE, the Concept 50, also shown at Detroit in 1989, was more adventurous. Concept 50 was more along the lines of what Mercury would offer if it was to come up with a stablemate to the Ford Probe. Concept 50 was designed by Ghia.

Concept 50 had no engine—it was a styling mockup—but it could be built with such innovative features as four-wheel drive and a multi-valve V-6 engine.

Ford vice president for design Jack Telnack said at the show, "1989 Ford concept cars contain two vehicles which were never intended to be shown to the public." The Concept 50 and the ONE were probably those two vehicles.

The Mercury ONE was conservatively styled, following the lines of the then-current Mercury Sable and Ford Taurus, but in a smaller format. ONE had an enlarged greenhouse, which was separated from the lower body by a strong black belt painted on the hood and rear deck. The bases of both front and rear windows were concave. *Ford Historical Collection*

Unlike the conservative ONE, the Concept 50 was more adventurous, designed along the lines of what Mercury would offer if it were to come up with a stablemate to the Ford Probe. Concept 50 was designed by Ghia. It had no engine—it was a styling mock-up—but it could be built with such innovative features as four-wheel drive and a multi-valve V-6 engine. *Ford Historical Collection*

1999 Marauder

The Marauder concept car could be defined as a Mercury Grand Marquis on steroids. It was trimmed down, pumped up, and ready for action, according to Mercury.

The Marauder was based on the 1999 Grand Marquis, with V-8 power and rear-wheel drive. Under the hood was a 4.6-liter SOHC sequential electronic fuel-injected V-8 with performance modifications. First, the engineers added a Ford SVO supercharger fed by a free-flowing K&N air filter. To relieve back pressure on the other end, a tuned 2.25-inch dual exhaust system was fabricated, exiting through a pair of polished 3-inch MEGS tips.

The Marauder chassis was tuned for more performance as well. First, Edelbrock Performer IAS shock absorbers were fitted, then a fat sway bar and a more aggressive wheel and tire

Marauder was based on the 1999 Grand Marquis, with V-8 power and rear-wheel drive. Under the hood was a 4.6-liter SOHC sequential electronic fuel injected V-8 with performance modifications. Engineers added a Ford SVO supercharger fed by a free-flowing K&N air filter. *Ford Historical Collection*

package. The Mercury design team selected Enkei SST-2 alloy wheels, 17x8 inches in the front and 18x8 inches in the rear, shod with Pirelli P-Zero performance radial tires; 245/50HR17s in the front and 255/50HR18s in the rear. The tire combination gave the Marauder an aggressive stance.

The exterior of the Marauder was finished with a monochromatic black. All extraneous trim was removed to further clean up the body lines. Night vision was augmented with a set of PIAA 1500XT fog lamps integrated into the front fascia. Inside, a pair of sporty buckets trimmed in supple leather replaced the Grand Marquis' standard bench seat. The standard column shift was replaced with a floor-mounted shifter in a custom center console. In place of the factory gauge package was a contemporary silver-faced gauge cluster, with the entire panel trimmed with a Satin Tech material.

1999 (my) Mercury

Designers and engineers spent a lot of time considering different ways to get people in and out of the (my) Mercury. The result of their efforts was what Ford Vice President of Design J. Mays called a "modern coupe" with a large rear hatch that swung up from a short tailgate. The hatch included the amber-colored back, side, and rear windows. The tailgate extended out to create a large cargo area behind the four bucket seats. The front doors swung open conventionally, but the rear doors were hinged at the back. The (my) Mercury was designed to combine maximum versatility with style. Up front, the aggressive bumper housed two large driving lamps and a rectangular grille. Trapezoidal headlights sat high above the grille to maximize the range. The four-wheel-drive concept car demonstrated one vision for a multi-activity vehicle that blurred the boundaries between a car, a truck, and a sport utility vehicle.

This Mercury was a "modern coupe" with a large rear hatch that swung up from a short tailgate. The hatch included the amber-colored back and side and rear windows. The tailgate extended out to create a large cargo area behind the four bucket seats. Front doors swung open conventionally, but rear doors were hinged at the back. *Ford Historical Collection*

The (my) Mercury was built on the design direction already established for Mercury by other concept and production vehicles. Its silhouette was formed with an arching roof and hard-edged rear hatch line, accented by precise, flared wheel housings to create a bold, solid ground stance.

The technical, highly machined look of the exterior was carried over to the interior with aluminumlike accents and exposed framework. The exposed sheet metal on the C-pillar was designed to create a sense of safety and security. Uniquely designed bucket seats were mounted on polished aluminum arched tracks that created open space under the seat for legroom or storage. The seats were leather-covered.

The front console featured an amber-colored mouse-like device that functioned as the control for the radio, climate control, and GPS. The display screen also was housed in the center of the dash, as were the tachometer, speedometer, and fuel gauge. Center mounting allowed for right-hand or left-hand drive.

The rear bucket seats folded down, and the floor of the cargo area extended over the back of the seats for a flat, expanded cargo space. With the rear tailgate extended, there was 6 feet of cargo area.

1999 Gametime Villager

Mercury's Gametime Villager concept car was created to make any stadium a homecoming party in the making.

Minivans are naturals for tailgate-type activities, and the Gametime concept took that theme to an extreme.

The basis for the Gametime was the Villager minivan, with a 3.3-liter SOHC V-6. The exterior styling was altered with the addition of new front and rear fascias and bolder body-side cladding. Two canvas sunroofs from Hollandia provided additional ventilation and were perfect for sunny days. The rear liftgate featured a fitted tent canopy to provide protection from the elements on classic fall football days. There was even a retractable satellite dish to pull in far-away games, so there was no need to even leave the driveway for a proper tailgate party.

The Gametime Villager was lowered with a set of Rousch racing springs at all four corners. Hand-cut 235/50R18 Michelin concept tires were mounted on TSW Hockenheim-R 18-inch alloy wheels.

Inside, the Gametime was trimmed in two-tone leather with Mercury logos embroidered on the seats. The interior storage space was abundant for ice chests, picnic tables and chairs, and a barbecue grille.

The most unique aspect was a built-in rear entertainment center that featured side-mounted stereo speakers, an ice bucket, a humidor, storage, and an integrated DVD player. Built into the module was a 21-inch flat-panel monitor, to view either the DVD or feed from the satellite dish.

Oldsmobile

Like Mercury, Oldsmobile's collection of dream cars has been primarily based on production models. But there have been notable exceptions.

Ed Welburn designed the Aerotech for Oldsmobile to showcase first the Quad 4 and, later, the Aurora engine. Other modern Olds dream cars have also been unlike any production cars, so it appears Olds designers are getting the green light to stretch their imaginations.

1953 Fiesta

The first Oldsmobile dream car was the 1953 Fiesta, built for that year's Motorama. The Fiesta was a convertible built on the 98 chassis but with a body that was almost 3 inches lower than the production 98. It had a number of other differences from the production car, including a wraparound windshield and a Rocket V-8 engine that developed 170 horsepower. A Hydra-Matic automatic transmission put the power to the wheels. The Fiesta also included power steering and brakes, a deluxe radio, heater defroster, Autronic Eye, whitewall tires, and backup lights. The Fiesta was so popular that Oldsmobile put the car into limited production, building 458 copies.

1953 Starfire convertible

Oldsmobile's second 1953 dream car was the fiberglass-bodied Starfire. This Corvette-like two-seater was named after the Lockheed F-94B Starfire fighter plane. Under the hood of this convertible was a specially built 308-cubic-inch Rocket V-8 rated at 200 horsepower, marking the first time this figure had been reached. The front-end treatment included a large oval grille that was used by Oldsmobile on

later production cars. The Starfire was painted turquoise with a turquoise and white leather interior.

1954 F-88

This two-door fiberglass convertible was a takeoff of the Corvette fiberglass body using an Olds drivetrain. It was built on a 102-inch wheelbase and was slightly more than 167 inches long. It was painted metallic gold with pigskin-colored upholstery. The instruments included a tachometer and chronometer. On the sides were two large "88"s. The high rear fenders of the F-88 terminated in two cone-shaped taillights, much like the Corvette. The exhaust outlets were integral with the lower rear fenders and had oval openings with decorative louvers just ahead of them on the lower fender panel. Seven vertical bumper guards were part of the rear bumper. The entire rear bumper unit dropped down to reveal the spare tire.

Under the hood of the F-88 was a 250-horsepower version of the 324-cubic-inch Rocket V-8. It had a 9:1 compression ratio. Power was transmitted to the wheels through a Hydra-Matic automatic transmission.

In 1957 the F-88 was modified for the show circuit again, this time adding quad headlights and small tailfins.

Oldsmobile's first dream car was the 1953 Fiesta, built for that year's Motorama. Fiesta was a convertible built on the 98 chassis but with a body that was almost three inches lower than the production 98. It also had a wraparound windshield and a Rocket V-8 engine that developed 170 horsepower. *Oldsmobile Historical Center*

Starfire was a Corvette-like two-seater that was named after the Lockheed F-94B Starfire fighter plane. Under the hood was a specially built 308 cubic inch Rocket V-8 rated at 200 horsepower, marking the first time this figure had been reached. *Oldsmobile Historical Center*

1954 Cutlass

The second 1954 dream car was the Cutlass, a name that would have a long history in Oldsmobile models. Like the Starfire, the Cutlass was named after a jet plane, this time the Chance-Vought Navy fighter Cutlass. The Oldsmobile version was painted metallic silver with a white and copper leather interior. The Cutlass was built on a 110-inch wheelbase and was 188 inches long. The styling touches included open front wheel housings, stacked exhausts under the taillights, and a "bubble" roof.

1955 Delta

Oldsmobile's only 1955 dream car was the Delta, which was a four-passenger coupe based on the 88. It was built on a 120-inch wheelbase and was only 53 inches high. The Delta was 201 inches long, 74 inches wide, and had a 6.2-inch ground clearance.

Among the styling touches were rear fender-mounted fuel tanks, aluminum wheels, and anodized aluminum trim. Interior features included four bucket seats and a center console that held the radio controls and provided storage. The rear armrest contained storage space and window controls. Two huge instrument pods, riding on a floating strut, faced the driver with the speedometer and tachometer, with the fuel gauge mounted between them. The instrument panel also included such accessories as a cigarette lighter,

padded cover, map pockets, convenience tray, and wide-angle rearview mirror, as well as a full-width speaker and air outlet combination.

Oldsmobile advertised the Delta by stating, "The Supersonic Shape Comes to Automobile Styling." Among the features highlighted in a company brochure were the wide-set ovals to house the headlamps and parking-driving lights, as well as the intake scoop that helped cool the front brakes. The brake drums were integral parts of the wheels.

Power came from a 250-horsepower Rocket V-8 engine with a 10.0:1 compression ratio. A Hydra-Matic Super Drive transmission was included. Engine exhaust exited through dual stacks located just under the rear bumper. They flanked the spare tire door and served as bumper guards. Wraparound taillights accented the fleetness of the car.

1956 Golden Rocket

Introduced at the 1956 Motorama in New York City, the Golden Rocket two-seater was built of reinforced plastic and painted bronze metallic. Inside, the seats were upholstered in blue and gold leather. Nerflike built-in bumpers replaced conventional bumpers.

The projectile-shaped bumper guards were incorporated into the front and rear fenders, giving the Golden Rocket an overall rocket effect, similar to the Cadillac Cyclone. This was fitting, because as Helen Earley and Jim Walkinshaw

This two-door fiberglass convertible was a takeoff on the Corvette fiberglass body using an Olds drivetrain. It was painted metallic gold with pigskin-colored upholstery. The high rear fenders of the F-88 terminated in two cone-shaped taillights, much like the Corvette. *Oldsmobile Historical Center*

wrote in their history of Oldsmobile, "Oldsmobile was partial to jet fighter names because of the Rocket [engine] name association."

To aid entry, whenever a door opened, the roof panel automatically rose, and the seat rose 3 inches and swiveled outward. The tilt steering wheel, one of the first, also aided entry. The plastic dorsal fins just to the rear of the doors on the fender crown line were lighted in red and served as running lights. The Golden Rocket was built on a 105-inch wheelbase and was 201 inches long and 49.5 inches tall.

Under the hood was a 234-cubic-inch Rocket V-8 that produced 275 horsepower on a 9.5:1 compression ratio.

1959 F-88 Mark III

The F-88 Mark III was a low, sleek two-seater that was Harley Earl's swan song. This car was bright red with a

Oldsmobile Historical Center

Cutlass was named after the Chance-Vought Navy fighter Cutlass. It was painted metallic silver with a white and copper leather interior. Cutlass was built on a 110-inch wheelbase and was 188 inches long. Styling touches included open front wheel housings, stacked exhausts under the tail lights and a bubble roof. *Oldsmobile Historical Center*

brushed-aluminum retractable hardtop. The 102-inch wheelbase carried a combination fiberglass and steel body that stood 46 inches tall. Inside were bucket seats and aircraft-style instruments featuring a rotating disc-type tachometer and speedometer, color-coded according to range. To obtain the low hood, there was a special carbure-tor arrangement and a modified crossflow aluminum radiator. The muffler/exhaust system was mounted ahead of the engine, exiting in front of the front wheels. An experimental Hydra-Matic transmission was mounted in the rear to improve weight distribution. Earl drove the Mark III for a while during his retirement.

Delta was a four-passenger coupe based on the 88. Among the styling touches were rear fender-mounted fuel tanks, aluminum wheels, and anodized aluminum trim. Interior features included four bucket seats and a center console that held the radio controls and provided storage. *Oldsmobile Historical Society*

The Golden Rocket two-seater was built of reinforced plastic and painted bronze metallic. Inside, the seats were upholstered in blue and gold leather. Conventional bumpers were replaced by nerflike built-in bumpers. *Oldsmobile Historical Center*

1962 X-215

After a few years without a new dream car—the F-88 Mark III was revised several times in the interim—Oldsmobile came out with the X-215 in 1962. This two-seater convertible was built on the new F-85 platform but had a fiberglass Thunderbird Sports Roadster-inspired tonneau panel behind the front seats. Incorporated into the tonneau was an airfoil-section roll bar. The tonneau cover also merged with the center console. The X-215 had a full-width concave grille, four headlamps, air intake scoops, and a rally-type windscreen. Air scoops mounted ahead of the rear wheels ducted fresh air to the rear brakes. The X-215 was painted Firefrost Silver, with a narrow black stripe running down the center.

The interior styling featured black leather upholstery on individual bucket seats. The instrument panel consisted of two dominant dials flanked by smaller gauges. The speedometer was in the large left dial, while there was a cluster of four accessory gauges in the right dial. A small tachometer was located to the left of the speedometer, and a turbo boost gauge was mounted on the right. In the center console were the glove box, an ashtray, and the T-handled shifter. Under the hood was a turbocharged 3.5-liter aluminum V-8 rated at 215 horsepower. It delivered its power to the rear wheels through a Hydra-Matic automatic transmission.

1962 J-TR

The J-TR was designed specifically for the 1963 Chicago Auto Show. This was a four-seater F-85 convertible with aluminum wheels, rectangular headlamps, louvered rocker panel moldings, stainless-steel exhaust headers, and four bucket seats. The aluminum wheels were visible through full fender openings. The exhaust pipes exited through louvered rocker panels.

The interior was custom-fitted with four bucket seats and a full-length console.

The F-88 Mark III was a low, sleek two-seater that was Harley Earl's swan song. This car was bright red with a brushed aluminum retractable hardtop. Inside were bucket seats and aircraft-style instruments featuring a rotating disc-type tachometer and speedometer, color-coded according to range. *Oldsmobile Historical Center*

Oldsmobile came out with the X-215 in 1962. This two-seater convertible was built on the new F-85 platform but had a fiberglass Thunderbird Sports Roadster-inspired tonneau panel behind the front seats. Incorporated into the tonneau was an airfoil-section rollbar. *Oldsmobile Historical Center*

Oldsmobile Historical Center

1963 El Torero

Based on the Oldsmobile 98, the El Torero was introduced at the Chicago Automobile Show in 1963. It was painted a Firefrost gold on the outside. The interior upholstery was patterned in a red-black-gold-and-white brocade on the door and side panels, console, and thin-shell bucket seats.

1964 4-4-2 Police Apprehender

This car was first shown at the Oldsmobile exhibits at the GM Futurama and New York World's Fair. The convertible was equipped with the new Police Apprehender package, including a 310-horsepower Jetfire Rocket V-8 engine, four-speed transmission, dual exhausts, and a 3.36:1 rear axle.

1968 Toronado Granturisimo

The Toronado provided the basis for this 1968 Oldsmobile dream car with the Toronado Granturisimo. This car featured fastback styling on a body that had 9 inches removed from the standard Toronado wheelbase. The overall height was also reduced by modifying the springs. Under the hood was a 475-cubic-inch V-8 with

J-TR was designed for the 1963 Chicago Auto Show. It was a four-seater F-85 convertible with aluminum wheels, rectangular headlamps, louvered rocker panel moldings, stainless steel exhaust headers, and four bucket seats. *Oldsmobile Historical Center*

three two-barrel Rochester carburetors. Among the innovations on this car were digital instruments, a safety warning system, special ventilation package, and four-overhead speakers for the sound system. It was painted electric blue.

1969 Apollo

This "space age" concept car was first shown at the 1969 New York International Automobile Show. The "capsule" was painted fireball red with black accent stripes and hood panels. The interior featured four metallic red and black leather contoured couches (like the Apollo moon capsule) with head restraints. While the paint and interior were specially prepared for shows, the basic body package was available on standard 4-4-2 convertibles that year.

1987 Aerotech ST

This sleek speed-record car was unveiled late in 1986 as a test bed for the new Oldsmobile Quad-4 engine. Chief engineer Ted Louckes was behind the Aerotech project. He said, "I thought we should demonstrate something about the engine so it would catch the eye of the public. What we

The Police Apprehender was first shown at the Oldsmobile exhibits at the GM Futurama and New York World's Fair. It was equipped with the new Police Apprehender package, including a 310 horsepower Jetfire Rocket V-8 engine, four-speed transmission, dual exhausts, and a 3.36:1 rear axle. *Oldsmobile Historical Center*

Toronado provided the basis for this 1968 Oldsmobile dream car, the Toronado Granturisimo, featured fastback styling on a body that was nine inches shorter than the standard Toronado. Among the innovations on this car were digital instruments, a safety warning system, special ventilation package, and a four-overhead speakers for the sound system. It was painted electric blue. *Oldsmobile Historical Center*

needed was a glamorous show car, something that is dynamite-looking, that would be a real engineering endeavor as far as aerodynamic performance."

The design staff and the engineering staff worked on parallel projects. Ed Welburn was the chief designer on the project. The goal was 235 miles per hour at Indianapolis from an 850-horsepower engine. Situations made running at Indianapolis impossible, so a new venue for the record setting was chosen. The new track was the six-mile Firestone test oval at Fort Stockton, Texas.

The version used for the Quad-4 record attempts was the ST, or short tail, version. Later, an LT, or long tail, version was also built.

Louckes asked long-time friend A. J. Foyt if he'd be interested in driving the car on the record attempt. Foyt agreed and set a new closed-course speed record of 257.123 miles per hour in August 1987. The next day, he drove the long-tail Aerotech to a new flying-mile record of 267.399 miles per hour.

In December 1992, the Aerotech LT was fitted with an essentially stock Aurora V-8 engine and taken to Fort Stockton. This time the car broke long-distance world records held by Mercedes-Benz for 10,000 and 25,000 kilometers with average speeds of 171 and 158 miles per hour, respectively. All told, the Aurora-engined Aerotech broke more than 45 world records in eight days of 24-hour-a-day driving.

1992 Anthem

Planned as a midsize car that would set Oldsmobile's course for the future, the Anthem four-door sedan incorporated a long wheelbase with short overhangs combined with a long cowl area to improve aerodynamics. With the extreme cab-forward design of the Anthem, the interior space was improved.

While viewed as a vision of the future, Anthem also incorporated many features found on then-contemporary Oldsmobile vehicles, such as a heads-up display, a Visual Information Center, and a Fluidic Air System that could defrost the large expanses of glass. Dennis Burke, head of Oldsmobile's Exterior 1 studio, said he felt the Anthem was an advanced Cutlass Supreme.

The glass roof had two liquid crystal diode panels. Located over the front and rear seats, the dials allowed passengers to vary the opacity of the glass from clear to completely opaque, depending on the solar load. With all glass panels

Aerotech was unveiled late in 1986 as a test bed for the new Oldsmobile Quad-4 engine. The version used for the Quad-4 record attempts was the ST, or short tail, version. Later, an LT, or long tail, version was also built. The Aerotech LT was fitted with an essentially stock Aurora V-8 engine and taken to Fort Stockton. *Oldsmobile Historical Center*

flush-mounted, Oldsmobile's Anthem sedan boasted a coefficient of drag of 0.26, which is considered world class for a midsize car.

Complementary tones of gray and beige leather highlighted the interior, creating a harmonious and refined appearance. The instrument panel swept into the door panels for continuity of design.

The driver's view was a grouping of simple and functional analog gauges. The controls were logically placed within easy sight and reach of the driver. Mounted between the driver's and front passenger's bucket seats was a pivoting reconfigurable screen that offered navigation information as well as a way to help the driver avoid traffic congestion. With this screen, the driver could also locate restaurants, hotels, and other local points of interest.

Under the long hood was a supercharged version of Oldsmobile's Quad 4 engine that generated 242 horsepower at 6,400 rpm. The engine drove the front wheels through a four-speed automatic transmission. A two-stroke 3.0-liter V-6 was offered as an alternate engine.

Oldsmobile Historical Center

Antares provided Oldsmobile a chance to build on the brand character themes it developed for the Aurora production car. These themes included the "shoulders" over the wheel arches, thin horizontal headlamps, 18-inch wheels, and a translucent rear taillight. Antares was 188.2 inches long, about 17 inches shorter than Aurora, yet the wheelbases were essentially identical at 113.4 inches. *Oldsmobile Historical Center*

Anthem. *Oldsmobile Historical Center*

1995 Antares

Introduced at the 1995 North American Auto Show in Detroit, the Antares provided Oldsmobile a chance to build on the brand character themes it developed for the Aurora production car. These themes were shown by "shoulders" over the wheel arches, thin horizontal headlamps, 18-inch wheels, and a translucent rear taillight. The Antares was 188.2 inches long, about 17 inches shorter than the Aurora, yet the wheelbases were essentially identical at 113.4 inches.

Inside, the Antares combined new materials and technologies. The seat belts were integrated with the seats, adding to comfort and freeing up B-pillar space for umbrella and ice scraper storage. The gauges were inspired by analog

(continued on page 129)

Color Gallery

Buick's 1951 XP-300 featured an all-aluminum body and a unique two-piece trunk. For the early 1950s, the car was extremely low, giving it a custom-car look. *John Heilig*

The 1951 Buick LeSabre looked like a jet fighter ready for takeoff. This car contained several unusual features, including a rain sensor and built-in hydraulic jacks to raise the car. *John Heilig*

PREVIOUS PAGE
The car that started it all—the 1938 Buick Y-Job. A product of the popular streamlining design movement in the 1930s, the Y-Job sported concealed headlights, copious amounts of bright speedlines along the fenders, and no running boards. All of these styling treatments gave the Y-Job a long, low, and wide stance. It was a look that was missing from most production cars of the time. *Buick Public Relations*

OPPOSITE PAGE
Two archival views of the Buick LeSabre show the influence of aircraft design. The rear fender fins and simulated turbine engine ports define the overall shape of the car. *John Heilig*

Buick's Centurion boasted a full transparent roof and a gadget-laden interior. From steering wheel to speedometer, nearly everything inside the Centurion was an experiment. *John Heilig*

Looking a bit like a 1953 Corvette, the 1954 Buick Wildcat II represented a new departure for Buick. Up until this car was created, Buick produced large, luxurious cars. With the Wildcat II, Buick experimented with small, sporty cars. *Buick Public Relations*

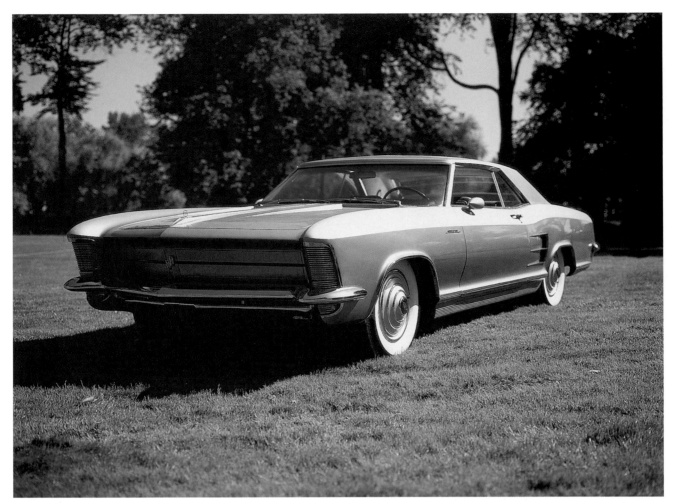

The Buick Riviera Silver Arrow appeared very much like the production Riviera of the early 1960s. However, the car was shorter and lower than the production model and featured special body and wheel treatments.
John Heilig

Resembling a 1950s Rambler convertible, Buick's Cielo four-door convertible featured unusual styling and sported many high-tech features to control various systems, including ignition.
Buick Public Relations

The rear-wheel-drive XP2000 four-door sedan. This concept car focused more on safety and comfort features than body design and engine technology. *Buick Public Relations*

The first Coupe de Ville was built on a Sixty Special 133-inch-wheelbase chassis. It had a Fleetwood body with a one-piece curved windshield, simulated scoops on the forward edges of the rear fenders, and chrome scuff plates below the doors. *Cadillac Historical Collection*

The Voyagé was a four-passenger test platform that allowed Cadillac engineers to develop and incorporate new features into automobiles that they were designing for the future. Voyagé's aerodynamic profile was outstanding, with a drag coefficient of just 0.28, making it one of the world's most aerodynamic gasoline-powered vehicles. *Cadillac Historical Collection*

The XP-700 was a Bill Mitchell–customized Corvette. The side cove contained three scoops to draw air out of the engine compartment. Up front, the extended nose contained an oval grille similar to a Ferrari 250GT, and even included a prancing horse medallion. *General Motors Historical Collection*

The Astro II was a mid-engined derivative of the XP-880, which in itself was an update of the XP-819. It still required wider rear wheels and tires. The entire rear section lifted to expose the engine. *General Motors Historical Collection*

The Express was described as a concept car for high-speed intercity travel. It showed dramatic aerodynamics, with one single surface from the front bumper back to the taillights. Its drag coefficient was a phenomenal 0.195. The Express was driven by a gas turbine engine, chosen because of its low-speed torque. *General Motors Historical Collection*

The Nomad sport wagon combined the performance and handling of a sport sedan with the access and flexibility of a sport utility vehicle. The Nomad was equipped with a small-block Chevrolet V-8 engine, independent rear suspension, and shift-by-wire transmission. Styling features included venetian blind–type slots that kicked up and slid forward, exposing a 36-inch opening in the roof. *General Motors Historical Collection*

Low-profile tires, sculpted front fenders, and a small fin on the trunk lid gave the Dodge Concept Car a sporty look. *Daimler Chrysler Historical Collection*

Unlike the old Dodge Charger of the 1960s, the 1990s Charger R/T was a four-door sedan. *Daimler Chrysler Historical Collection*

The new Dodge Power Wagon borrowed and updated styling features found on the original Power Wagon of the 1940s. Protruding fenders, a louvered hood, and an aggressive stance gave the Power Wagon a bold, rugged attitude. *Daimler Chrysler Historical Collection*

The 1994 Mustang Mach III was created to celebrate the thirtieth anniversary of Ford's original Mustang. *Ford Historical Collection*

The Oldsmobile Anthem four-door sedan featured highly sculpted body sides and a very streamlined surface from front to rear. *Oldsmobile Historical Center*

The Jeep Jeepster combined the performance and sportiness of a road car with the durability and ruggedness of an off-road vehicle. *Daimler Chrysler Historical Collection*

Oldsmobile's Recon used and enhanced the basic styling features of several contemporary Oldsmobile models. By incorporating these elements, the Recon sport utility vehicle was readily identified as an Oldsmobile. *Oldsmobile Historical Center*

The mid-engined, plastic-bodied Plymouth Pronto Spyder. *Daimler Chrysler Historical Collection*

The 1987 Pontiac Pursuit featured fully enclosed wheels and a streamlined body. *John Heilig*

Pontiac's 1988 Banshee was constructed of a tube chassis and fiberglass skin. To keep the body aerodynamic, the glass was fit flush, and the exterior door handles and mirrors were eliminated. *John Heilig*

The design of the Recon sharpened the forms of then-current Oldsmobile products such as Aurora, Intrigue, and Alero. Its unique shape emphasized Oldsmobile design elements such as wheel-oriented shoulders, lower body side fluting, and horizontal headlights. The vehicle's ASC-designed two-panel power sunroof extended over both front and rear passengers. *Oldsmobile Historical Center*

(continued from page 112)

watches, and there was mahogany wood trim. The interior air was controlled by oscillating fans hidden behind mesh-covered areas on the instrument panel and at the side and rear of the center console. The console also contained a pop-up Guidestar navigation system that used onboard computers, dead reckoning, and satellite technology.

1999 Recon

The design of the Recon was an evolution of then-current Oldsmobile products such as the Aurora, the Intrigue, and the Alero, but instead of using soft forms it sharpened them. Its unique shape emphasized Oldsmobile design elements such as wheel-oriented shoulders, lower-body side fluting, and horizontal headlights. The vehicle's ASC-designed two-panel power sunroof extended over both front and rear passengers. All-wheel drive and Michelin extended mobility tires were a part of the package.

Inside the Recon, flat-panel displays were located front and rear for access to an information/entertainment system called "infotainment." Personal information could be loaded into the system using a Personal Digital Assistant (PDA). *Yahoo! Internet Life* called the Recon, "A fully wired road machine with dash-mounted lap-top ports and Net access."

The instrument panel could also be reconfigured using display windows similar to those on PCs. It featured access to real-time traffic information as well as navigation assistance. The on-board communications center included a hands-free cell phone with voice mail and e-mail capability. Other features of the Recon interior included a rotary shifter and a totally keyless ignition.

The rear console was reconfigurable and featured a flip-and-fold design. Seats, designed by Lear Corp., had no covering or padding and used a high-tech lightweight material that would not fade or scratch. Their thin profile provided more passenger and storage space.

CHAPTER 11

Plymouth

Virgil Exner designed some of his most magnificent creations for Plymouth. When Exner backed the XX-500, Explorer Special, and Belmont, he was at the top of his profession, throwing a small scare at Harley Earl with his finned designs of the 1950s.

The modern Pronto and Pronto Spyder show that the present generation of Chrysler designers don't have to take a back seat to the legendary Exner. In fact, it might have been interesting if Tom Gale and John Herlitz were contemporary with Exner to see who had the better designs.

1951 XX-500

The first of Plymouth's postwar concept cars was the XX-500, which was built by Ghia in Italy and designed by that firm's Mario Boano and Luigi Segre. Virgil Exner, who had been named chief of design in 1952, was not involved directly with this one. It was based on the standard 1951 Plymouth chassis with a wheelbase of 118.5 inches and the standard 217.8-cubic-inch, 97-horsepower inline-six under the hood. The gearbox was a three-speed manual.

The XX-500 wasn't a radically designed car. It was tame even by Ghia's standards. The four-door sedan did have smooth rounded lines that were unusual for a car of the era. It resembled Pininfarina's Cisitalia coupe, even though Ghia built the XX-500. Inside, the upholstery was Bedford Cord and leather. The whole car only cost $10,000 to put together, which was a bargain even in 1951.

"It was brought over by Ghia," Virgil Exner Jr. told Richard Langworth in *Special-Interest Autos*, "to show Chrysler their ability and craftsmanship and to get Chrysler to give them some business. In retrospect, the XX-500 was

pretty dumpy, but it was built along the lines of what they were doing in Italy at the same time. The design didn't scale up too well, but it started the whole idea in dad's mind that they could do an advanced design and build it as a real car, as opposed to just mock-ups as in this country."

Approval of the XX-500 project inspired Exner Sr. to set up a small staff to create dream cars for Chrysler. The staff consisted of 17 people, including four designers and several model builders.

1954 Explorer Special

Ghia's next Plymouth concept car was the Explorer. Unlike the sport utility of today from Ford with the same name, the 1954 Plymouth Explorer was a smooth two-door sports coupe. Called an "idea car" by Plymouth, the Explorer resembled the Dodge Firearrow Sport Coupe, with a few exceptions. First, the Dodge was a four-seater, while the Plymouth was a two-seater, with the rear area was occupied by fitted luggage. The large grille of the Explorer was not unlike that shown on the XX-500, indicating that Plymouth thought Ghia had a good thing going.

The Explorer was built on a 114-inch wheelbase and used the standard inline-six, now rated at 110 horsepower.

The first of Plymouth's postwar concept cars was the XX-500, which was built by Ghia in Italy. Although the four-door sedan wasn't a radically designed car, it did have smooth rounded lines that were unusual for a car of the era. It resembled Pininfarina's Cisitalia coupe, even though Ghia built the XX-500.
Daimler Chrysler Historical Collection

The 1954 Plymouth Explorer was a smooth two-door sports coupe. It resembled the Dodge Firearrow Sport coupe, with a few exceptions. First, the Dodge was a four-seater, the Plymouth a two-seater, with the rear area occupied by fitted luggage. The large grille of the Explorer was not unlike that shown on the XX-500, indicating that Plymouth thought Ghia had a good thing going. *Daimler Chrysler Historical Collection*

The engine was attached to a Hy-Drive automatic transmission, which detracted from overall performance. Plymouth advertising bragged, "The Explorer exhibits the same outstanding performance and handling ease as its popular cousin, the new 1954 Hy-Style Plymouth."

The unique features of the Explorer were the exhaust pipes—which exited just below the taillights—a wraparound windshield, and recessed directional lights fitted into the front of the rub rail. The front end was cleaner than the Firearrow as well, with dual headlights recessed into the fascia. The sculptured side profile featured a rise over the rear wheels. The ads read, "Its graceful proportions are rakishly accented by sharply creased fenders and a low, flat hoodline."

The special features of the Plymouth Explorer included eggshell white aviation-style seats edged in black, fitted luggage, and radio controls that disappeared when they weren't needed.

1954 Belmont

The Belmont was not built by Ghia, but by Briggs Body. Al Pranz, chief designer for Briggs, styled it. Even though it was labeled a Plymouth, Belmont used a Dodge chassis, which gave it more length than the Explorer despite using the same wheelbase. Under the sleek hood was Dodge's V-8 that turned out 150 horsepower. The Belmont was built on a 114.0-inch wheelbase, was 191.5 inches long, 73.3 inches wide, and 49.3 inches tall.

Painted a light metallic blue, the fiberglass Belmont had an oval chrome grille with a huge hood scoop that made it look something like an Austin-Healey 3000. Inside, the upholstery was white leather. Between the front seats was a console that contained controls for the radio and electric antenna. The spare tire and removable top occupied the trunk; luggage was carried behind the seats. The front wheel openings were fully cut out, while the rears were "half skirted," with flat tops that concealed the tire tops.

1956 Plainsman

The Plainsman, a station wagon concept car designed by Maury Baldwin of Chrysler, debuted in 1956. The Plainsman had several features that saw their way into production, including pointy rear tailfins and a grille that resembled that of the future Imperial. It also incorporated a rear-facing third seat, a spare tire located inside a fender well, and a vinyl-covered roof. Under the hood was a 260-cubic-inch V-8 that delivered something like 160 horsepower.

The two-door Plainsman was painted metallic beige, with a brown and white "unborn calfskin" interior. Among the other goodies were hydraulically activated steps that would provide access to the rear seat, front seats that had adjustable backs, and an air intake in the roof.

1958 Cabana

Another station wagon concept vehicle was the 1958 Cabana, which came from Ghia with pointy tailfins and a glass rear quarter to the "station wagon" portion of the body. Built on a 124-inch wheelbase, the Cabana didn't have a drivetrain, making it easier for the designers to be creative. It was painted metallic green and had matching green leather upholstery.

A four-door hardtop wagon, Chrysler stated its objectives in designing the vehicle as "(1) combine all desirable station wagon convenience features in one original body; (2) design for ambulance or hearse conversion; and (3) reduce the boxy squared-off rear-end appearance of contemporary station wagons."

1960 XNR

Virgil Exner finally got into the dream car act with the self-named 1960 XNR. Here was a two-seat sports car with a fixed headrest behind the driver's seat that rose into a single tailfin. The XNR was powered by a modified 225-cubic-inch Slant Six that could develop as much as 250 horsepower. The top speed was 135 miles per hour with Exner driving; 150 with a race car driver behind the wheel.

Virgil Exner Jr. told *Special-Interest Autos*, "We took it to the road test people after we had shown it around a bit. The laboratory really hopped up the engine to 250 horsepower, a tremendous amount of power. We took it to the proving grounds and had a professional drive it. He lapped at 151 or 152, which wasn't bad at that time."

Exner built the wedge-shaped XNR on a Valiant chassis, giving that chassis the most aerodynamic body it would ever see. Its most distinctive feature was an asymmetrical hood bulge that grew as it passed through the windshield plane and ended up as the driver's headrest. Where the headrest fin intersected the rear bumper an asymmetrical cross was formed.

The grille and front bumper were combined into a simple oval, with protection around the outside of the grille. Exner continued the asymmetrical theme by covering the passenger side of the car with a metal tonneau when it wasn't occupied. In front of the driver was a racing windscreen. The passenger's windscreen popped up when the seat was in use.

Rumor has it that the red and black XNR was purchased by the Shah of Iran after the Geneva International Auto Show. It has since disappeared.

Belmont was not built by Ghia, but by Briggs Body. Even though it was labeled a Plymouth, Belmont used a Dodge chassis, which gave it more length than Explorer despite using the same wheelbase. Painted a light metallic blue, the fiberglass Belmont had an oval chrome grille with a huge hood scoop that made it look something like an Austin-Healey 3000. *Daimler Chrysler Historical Collection*

Plainsman was a station wagon concept car with a couple of features that saw their way into production, including pointy rear tailfins and a grill that resembled that of the future Imperial. It also incorporated a rear-facing third seat, a spare tire located inside a fender well, and a vinyl-covered roof. *Daimler Chrysler Historical Collection*

Cabana came from Ghia with pointy tailfins and a glass rear quarter to the "station wagon" portion of the body. Built on a 124-inch wheelbase, Cabana didn't have a drivetrain, making it easier for the designers to be creative. It was painted metallic green and had matching green leather upholstery. *Daimler Chrysler Historical Collection*

1961 Valiant Asymmetrica

Following the asymmetrical XNR was the 1961 Valiant Asymmetrica. Also built on a Valiant chassis, this car had a huge oval grille with mesh cloth and a hood bulge that grew softly to the windshield. There was no "extension" of the bulge on the rear deck and, therefore, no driver's headrest. This was the last of Exner's concept cars.

1964 Satellite Landau

This car was a slightly modified version of the 1964 Satellite, with a flying buttress C-pillar that acted like a pseudo roll bar. After this vehicle, Plymouth's exotic show cars disappeared until the Prowler emerged some 30 years later.

"Since we got back seriously into doing concept cars in 1983, we've done about 40," said John Herlitz, Chrysler vice president of design. "All exist." Among those concept cars is one that made it into production, but it's the type of vehicle that the "new" Chrysler Corporation used to both stretch the envelope of car design and simultaneously see if the public would be interested in buying such a vehicle. We're talking, of course, about the Prowler.

1995 Back Pack

Introduced at the North American International Auto Show in Detroit, the Back Pack was designed for a youth-oriented niche. It was part sport utility, part pickup, and part sporty coupe. It was shorter than the Neon compact car, on which it was based, but as tall as a Voyager minivan. Under the hood was the 2.0-liter 16-valve-four of the Neon. The front suspension incorporated MacPherson struts, while the rear was an independent multilink design with Chapman struts. The driver's seat could convert into an office with a one-quarter turn of the seat. The passenger seat could fold flat to create a flat work surface with room for a mobile fax or laptop computer.

Virgil Exner finally got into the dream car act with the self-named 1960 XNR, a two-seat sports car with a fixed headrest behind the driver's seat that rose into a single tailfin. XNR was powered by a modified 225 cubic inch Slant Six that could develop as much as 250 horsepower. Top speed was 135 miles per hour with Exner driving; 150 with a race car driver behind the wheel. *Daimler Chrysler Historical Collection*

Following the asymmetrical XNR was the Valiant Asymmetrica, also built on a Valiant chassis. This car had a huge oval grille with mesh cloth and a hood bulge that grew softly to the windshield. *Daimler Chrysler Historical Collection*

Back Pack was designed for a youth-oriented niche. It was part sport utility, part pickup, and part sporty coupe. It was shorter than the Neon compact car, on which it was based, but as tall as a Voyager minivan. Under the hood was the 2.0-liter 16-valve four of the Neon. *Daimler Chrysler Historical Collection*

The Back Pack had a sports rack for bikes or skis, and had integral roof fork attachments and bed-mounted tire depressions and security straps to keep articles in place when the vehicle was moving. Secure cargo could be stored in a lockable trunk under the bed.

1997 Pronto

The Pronto was designed to give buyers a look at what a future five-door, four-passenger sedan might look like. The Pronto distinguished itself by its tall architecture, spacious interior, roll-back fabric roof, and distinctive standalone bumpers. The tall architecture seated passengers higher in

the vehicle to give them more of a "command-of-the-road feeling." Moving the windshield forward and using minimal front and rear overhang created additional interior space. The front grille had a look that was intentionally Prowler-like.

The front seats were buckets, while the rear seats were split-back fold-down. Rear bench seats were designed to fold flat, creating a large rear cargo area.

While the Pronto was constructed of traditional materials, the intent of the car was to use all-composite plastic with molded-in color to form the body. The body panels would be made of Acrylonitrile/Styrene/Acrylate (ASA)

Pronto was designed to give buyers a look at what a future five-door, four-passenger sedan might look like. The tall architecture seated passengers higher in the vehicle to give them more of a "command-of-the-road feeling." Moving the windshield forward and using minimal front and rear overhang created additional interior space. The front grille had a look that was intentionally Prowler-like. *Daimler Chrysler Historical Collection*

plastic and have a single molded-in color to simplify assembly and eliminate the painting process.

"With Pronto, we explored what a vehicle might look like if we used injection-molded plastic to construct it," said Walling. The vehicle was 148.8 inches long on a 101.0-inch wheelbase, 64.7 inches wide, and 58.0 inches tall. Power came from a 2.0-liter SOHC-four rated at 132 horsepower.

1998 Pronto Spyder

The Pronto Spyder borrowed a materials application from its cousin, the 1997 Pronto, first shown at the North American International Auto show in Detroit. It also had a relationship to Chrysler's Composite Concept Vehicle (CCV) shown at the 1997 Frankfurt Motor Show. The midengined sports roadster was built of polyethylene terephthalate (PET), the same material used to make plastic drinking bottles. Tom Tremont, chief designer for

Pacifica, Chrysler's West Coast design studio in Carlsbad, California, said, "PET technology has the potential to reduce manufacturing costs by 80 percent over conventional methods using steel."

In the engine compartment of the Pronto Spyder was a 2.4-liter dual overhead cam supercharged four-cylinder engine that produced 225 horsepower. It was matched to a five-speed manual transmission that was borrowed from the Neon racing program. This engine was mounted transversely behind the seats and in front of the rear wheels. The Pronto Spyder had 18-inch cast-aluminum wheels and was shod in 225/40R18 Goodyear tires.

Some of the classic elements of the Pronto Spyder included gauges that evoked the quality of Swiss watches; special taillamps with neon tubes that provided a softer, more even light; leather racing shell seats; a tortoiseshell steering wheel rim and "banjo spoke design"; tortoiseshell and chrome

Pronto Spyder borrowed a materials application from its cousin, the 1997 Pronto. It also had a relationship to Chrysler's Composite Concept Vehicle (CCV) shown at the 1997 Frankfurt Motor Show. The mid-engined sports roadster was built of polyethylene terephthalate (PET). In the engine compartment of the Pronto Spyder was a 2.4-liter dual overhead cam supercharged four-cylinder engine that produced 225 horsepower. *Daimler Chrysler Historical Collection*

treatments on the shifter knob; and a wraparound windshield like those found on sports racers of the 1950s.

"An injection mold process allows us to do razor sharp edges, precise intersections and incised names and details," Tremont said at the car's introduction. "These forms are pure, precise, simple and honest. In contrast to the body's 'machine-like' design, we blend romantic detailing in the interior that hints at an earlier classic sports racer era."

1999 Voyager XG

Chrysler designed the Plymouth Voyager XG mini-van for "Generation X," the active generation. "We built the Voyager XG concept minivan for the adventure-seeking, mountain-biking, trail-riding, ocean-surfing individual who has a lot of equipment and is always on the go," said Ralph Sarotte, DaimlerChrysler's general product manager—Minivan Platform. "The vehicle would expand the minivan market segment by attracting a new generation of minivan buyers.

The Voyager XG was powered by a 2.5-liter turbo diesel engine with enhanced output and a five-speed manual transaxle. The engine developed 115 horsepower and was capable of 33 miles per gallon on the highway and 22 miles in the city.

Painted in Starbrite Silver Metallic Clear coat with dark silver accents, the Voyager XG had a high-tech, expressive appearance. Similar to high-quality ski goggles and sunglasses, the Voyager XG's side and rear windows were reflective and coated with a blue tint. The vehicle had the Plymouth Prowler's 17-inch wheels, which were painted Sterling Silver with anodized blue center caps.

Inside, the spacious taupe interior featured leather seats with a high-tech fabric that had a woven metal appearance.

The interior was laden with storage cargo nets between the seats, rear headliner, passenger-side rear quarter, and behind all of the seats.

Other interior features included a power retractable cloth roof and a removable mobile storage pod that served as a built-in ice chest and storage drawer.

The Voyager XG was built on a 113.3-inch wheelbase and was 186.3 inches long, 76.8 inches wide, and 68.5 inches tall.

PONTIAC

presents the pattern for tomorrow.

Bonneville Special

The Bonneville Special, a low, racy-looking sports car, carries the traditional Silver Streak of Pontiac. This car of the future, built for experimental and show purposes only, is 48½ inches high and 158.3 inches in over-all length. Its plastic "bubble" canopy is hinged and counterbalanced for easy entrance. The Bonneville is powered by a high-output Pontiac eight.

Pontiac

Ever since John DeLorean transformed Pontiac in the 1960s, the brand has been GM's hot rod division. Early Pontiac dream car designs, such as the Banshee, reinforced this image. And while the brand has included a few practical vehicles in its dream car portfolio, there are still the hot rods.

Modern dream cars like the Rageous, GTO, and 300 GPX show that Pontiac hasn't lost any of its hot rod heritage, and apparently has no intention of losing it in the future.

1954 Bonneville Special

Paul Gillan and Homer LaGassey did the Bonneville Special and Strato-Streak show cars and the 1955 Pontiac with the double Silver Streaks on the hood. When McLean took the Firebird I project, that left Gillan and LaGassey without a show car. So they devised some additional sketches. One sketch turned out to be the Strato-Streak, the four-door B-pillarless sedan. The doors swung on the A- and C-pillars.

"Then we did the Bonneville Special show car," LaGassey told *Collectible Automobile*. "We put the Bonneville name on it because someone had been to the Bonneville Speedway and liked the name. That's where the thing came from. Not that we were geniuses. It just all fell in line."

Paul Gillan related this story to *Automobile Quarterly*: "I was running the Pontiac studio at the time. . . . Mr. Earl thought Pontiac was a fuddy-duddy outfit. [So he] decided it would be a good idea for Pontiac to have a car that was not conservative. He wanted to do something for Pontiac's racing image. So he came up with the idea of doing a Le Mans–type car, and insisted it had to be *short*. It had to be

maneuverable. That made for a very small car compared to most others of that time."

The Bonneville was a two-seater with definite Corvette overtones. The copper-colored plexiglass-roofed sports car had an aluminum-headed straight-eight engine with four Holley YH side-draft carburetors. It sported the classic Pontiac twin streaks on the hood and gullwing-style doors in the plexiglass roof. The instruments (picked up at an aircraft salvage yard) were arrayed across the dash, with six small instruments spread between the center and right and the tachometer and speedometer in front of the driver in a single nacelle.

"Something that [Earl] did want were those imitation oil coolers on the front fenders," Gillan continued. "They were machined from solid aluminum. And he wanted the Pontiac silver streaks, of course, for identity. Now about the spare tire on the back: That's what Mr. Earl wanted. He'd tried putting a Continental spare on the first Corvette when he and Bob McLean did that car as a Motorama job. He was sort of imitating the old MG. . . ."

1956 Club de Mer

Introduced at the 1956 GM Motorama, the Club de Mer was a low, two-passenger sports car that had a brushed

The Bonneville Special was a two-seater with definite Corvette overtones. The copper-colored plexiglass-roofed sports car had an aluminum-headed straight-eight engine with four Holley YH side-draft carburetors. It sported the classic Pontiac twin streaks on the hood and gullwing-style doors in the plexiglass roof. *John Heilig*

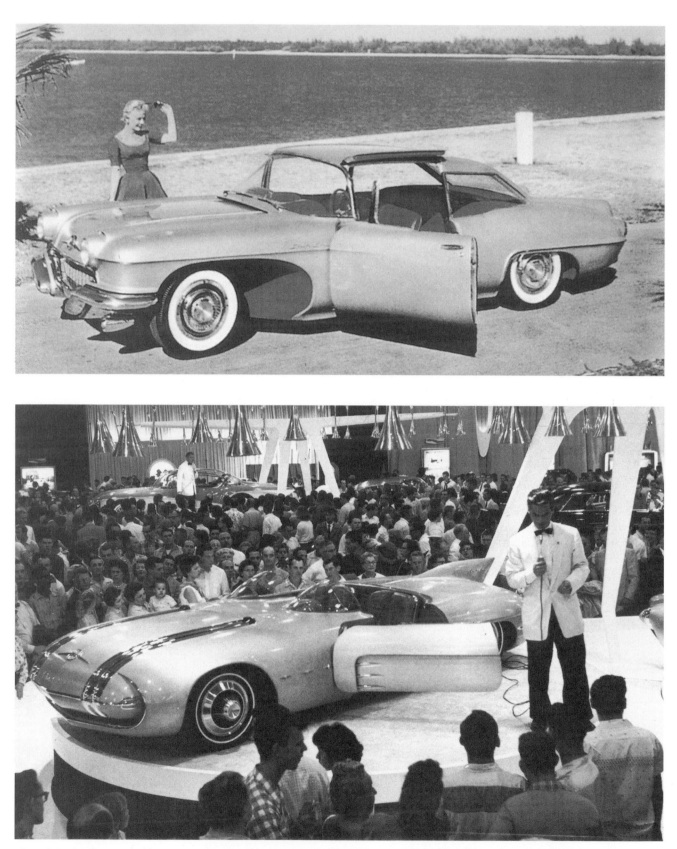

The Club de Mer was a low, two-passenger sports car that had a brushed anodized aluminum body. It was equipped with a 300 horsepower Pontiac Strato Streak V-8 engine. The synchromesh transmission was mounted behind the passenger compartment and connected with a special rear suspension. The exterior body color was Cerulean Blue, while the interior was finished in vermillion red leather. *John Heilig*

Trans Sport was the answer to a designer's dream assignment: develop a new multipurpose concept vehicle from the ground up to showcase ideas that could be functional and producible in the future. Trans Sport had a fluid aerodynamic shape with the functionality of a minivan. *John Heilig*

anodized aluminum body. The Club de Mer was equipped with a 300-horsepower Pontiac Strato Streak V-8 engine. It stood 38.4 inches tall to the top of the windshield and was 180.1 inches long. Built on a 104-inch wheelbase, the Club de Mer was 69.7 inches wide with a track of 56 inches in the front and 54 in the rear. It had 5 inches of ground clearance. The synchromesh transmission was mounted behind the passenger compartment and connected with a special rear suspension. This arrangement was chosen to allow for greater legroom for the driver and passenger.

The exterior body color was Cerulean Blue, while the interior was finished in vermillion red leather. The car's most striking feature was the dorsal fin that flashed up from the rear deck surface. According to Pontiac, the fin added fleetness to the car's appearance and also functioned as a stabilizing influence during operation. The twin bubble windshields, designed to deflect the wind upward, protected passengers.

At the nose of the Club de Mer was the air intake aperture for engine cooling. This chrome-lined opening engulfed the lower section of the front end. The highway

Banshee resurrected a dream car name Pontiac had used in 1962. Banshee's exterior was constructed of a fiberglass skin over a tubular frame and had a sleek, sloped profile and smooth-flowing sides with no interruptions. All glass was flush-mounted, as were the doors. There were no door handles or exterior mirrors. *John Heilig*

1988 Pontiac Banshee. *John Heilig Collection*

Banshee concept drawing. *John Heilig Collection*

and parking lights were brought together in a dual arrangement, one over the other. The entire lamp unit was designed so that when it wasn't in use it would revolve and disappear into the body, leaving a completely smooth front surface. Excessive engine heat was removed through outlet ports located on the sides of the front fenders.

1962 XP-833 Banshee

The Banshee was Corvette inspired and led to the design of the 1967 Firebird. This Banshee, unlike an earlier XP-833, had a V-8 engine. The earlier car had a six. It was originally designed to sell for $200 less than a stripped Corvette. It was built on a 90-inch wheelbase and was 167.7 inches long. It weighed about 2,200 pounds. A unique feature of the Banshee is its two-way trunk hinging. It was hinged at the back to lift like a Corvette and the tonneau would lift to store the top. It would also hinge at the front if you wanted to use it like a normal trunk and store luggage in it. William T. Collins Jr. was the head of the Banshee project. John S. DeLorean was the head designer.

Banshee interior. *John Heilig Collection*

1962 X-400

Conservatively styled, the X-400 had four rectangular headlamps protected by flip-up wire grilles. Under the hood was a supercharged 6.5-liter engine that delivered 500 horsepower. A pair of grille vents was added to the hood to provide air to the supercharger. They were labeled with big letters to let passersby know what was underneath. The performance wasn't stirring, with a top speed of less than 100 miles per hour. This sluggishness may have been caused by the X-400's curb weight of 4,850 pounds.

The X-400 was painted red and white. Inside, the seats were upholstered in red and white leather, with bucket seats for the driver and front passenger. The console between the seats held two levers: one for the shifter and one for the exhaust silencer.

1962 Monte Carlo

This Monte Carlo was unlike the Chevrolet production cars of later years. Pontiac built a high-performance two-door two-seater coupe. Based on the Tempest, it had a wheelbase that was 15 inches shorter than the production Tempest cars at 97 inches, and an overall length of 175 inches. It was powered by a supercharged 3.2-liter four-cylinder engine and had a four-speed manual transmission.

The interior styling was highlighted by two leather-covered bucket seats separated by a brushed aluminum console that ran the length of the interior. It used a stock Tempest instrument panel but added a tachometer and vacuum gauge.

1986 Trans Sport

The Trans Sport was the answer to a designer's dream assignment—develop a new multipurpose concept vehicle from the ground up to showcase ideas that could be functional and producible in the future. In fact, the Trans Sport minivan did make it into production as one of three General Motors "Dustbuster" minivans that differed from the concept vehicle.

The Trans Sport had a fluid aerodynamic shape with the functionality of a minivan. It was based on a front-wheel-drive sedan configuration extended to a 116-inch

Stinger was classified as a sport-style vehicle. It was a car with a Pontiac personality and roadability. Its aggressive exterior styling was made up of carbon-fiber panels. The glass panels, except for the windshield, were all removable. The gray-and-green body could be transformed from two-door enclosed transportation to open-air fun and was adaptable to a number of different activities. *John Heilig*

wheelbase, which was the length of a full-size wagon. These elements allowed the central floor to be extremely long and low. With an overall exterior height of 59.6 inches, the Trans Sport was 5 to 12 inches shorter than many minivan/wagon entries of the era. Still, it had an interior walk-through height of 48 inches, which was nearly equal to the competition. It also had a 12.5-inch step-in height and passenger accessibility that approached that of a mid-size sedan.

Terry Henline, Pontiac's exterior design studio chief, said the Trans Sport was a unique opportunity for Pontiac. "It was our chance to demonstrate the kind of freewheeling innovation you would expect from a totally new breed at Pontiac," he said.

The Trans Sport used a generous amount of glass with the front windshield extending well back over the driver. The driver's seating position was elevated for improved visibility. The side windows also wrapped into the roof, resulting in an interior headliner that was only 3 feet wide. The door handles were recessed into the structure of the door, and the composite headlamps were narrow openings containing five square units. The taillamps used a unique optical system that displayed red, amber, or clear backup modes. The right passenger door opened in "gull wing" style rather than sliding or hinging.

The minivan was powered by a 2.9-liter turbocharged V-6 aluminum engine that was not offered on any production models. Special 17x8-inch wheels with low aspect ratio P255/50VR17 tires completed the package.

The 1990 Sunfire was a four-person subcompact sporty coupe that was powered by a 2.0-liter 16-valve DOHC turbocharged inline four that produced 190 horsepower. Carbon fiber body panels composed the car. The doors were special two-part affairs featuring shorter, conventional front doors and two half-size rear doors, which opened from the front to rear to allow easier entry and exit. *John Heilig*

The two-seater Sunfire speedster was not part of the Sunfire product line. In fact, the Speedster was closer to the 1990 Sunfire concept car than it was to the production car. Both concept cars featured a wide-track, ground-hugging stance with aggressively styled exteriors. The aggressive exterior flowed effortlessly into the organic interior, which featured high-gloss Sunfire Mango-painted surfaces with dark sienna and graphite leather appointments. *John Heilig*

1987 Pursuit

"We were given the basic functions of the concept car—four-wheel drive, four-wheel steer, front engine, four-passenger capacity," said Pursuit project designer Dave Ross. The result was the 1987 Pursuit. The Pursuit was a "one box" aerodynamic coupe with sharply sloped front and rear windshields and a greenhouse that wrapped around the car.

The Pursuit's four wheels were more fully enclosed than any other General Motors car up to that time, with the possible exception of the Chevrolet Express, which was introduced at the same time. The lower edge of the body panel is low at the front wheel. It rises in a slight arch through the "Coke bottle" midsection of the car and returns to essentially ground level just in front of the rear wheel. *Car Styling* magazine noted that while most concept cars exaggerate the

wheel to a certain extent, in the Pursuit the wheels have "an undeniable lack of presence," especially the front wheels.

Power for the Pursuit came from a 2.0-liter 16-valve turbocharged-four, mounted transversely and horizontally to allow for the low front hood height.

The taillights were integrated into a shape that began at the door handles and continued around to the trunk surface. The lights were designed to glow red at night and when the vehicle was under braking, amber at the outside ends for turn signals and emergency flashers, and white at the inboard ends for backup illumination.

Pursuit's interior was driver-oriented and wrapped around the pilot. In front of the driver was a "driver/vehicle interface unit" that the driver used to steer the vehicle and operate its controls. Handgrip controls were used instead of a steering wheel. These had switches in the center and in the thumb area. With four-wheel steering limiting the lock-to-lock turning angle to 180 degrees, the driver would have been able to operate all the controls without releasing his grip on the interface unit.

The instrumentation included three cathode ray tubes and a heads-up display. The center CRT contained the tachometer and the telephone/travel guide/calendar system. The two flanking CRTs displayed gauges and also served as rearview mirrors, displaying the results of two small video cameras in the rear corners of the Pursuit.

All four passengers had four-point harnesses. The front passenger seat back pivoted toward the center console to facilitate rear seat entry. The rear seat itself featured an integrated child safety seat that would fold out of the rear seat back.

1988 Banshee

Presented as a sports car concept for the 1900s, the Banshee resurrected a dream car name Pontiac had used in

1994 Sunfire Speedster. *John Heilig Collection*

1962. Like its namesake, the 1988 Banshee was a futuristic performance coupe with realistic design and engineering features that could appear in later generations of the popular Firebird series. The exterior was constructed of a fiberglass skin over a tubular frame and had a sleek, sloped profile and smooth-flowing sides with no interruptions. All glass was flush-mounted, as were the doors. There were no door handles or exterior mirrors. The doors were opened by an infrared signal activated by pushing a button on a small, wristwatch-size device. The Banshee measured 201 inches long and 80 inches wide on a 105-inch wheelbase. It stood 46.25 inches high.

Although it had the appearance of a midengined car, the Banshee was powered by a front mounted port fuel-injected 4.0-liter DOHC aluminum V-8 that featured an integral block-head design for efficient air passage and engine breathing. Capable of producing 230 horsepower, the rear-wheel-drive sports coupe had a five-speed manual transmission, independent rear suspension, four-wheel anti-lock disc brakes, and wraparound adjustable rear spoilers. The wheels were 17 inches front and rear.

Inside, the Banshee had an operational heads-up display that projected a holographic image of the vehicle's speed, fuel level, turn signal information, and more. Also projected just below the HUD image was a virtual image display (VID) that showed an optically enlarged image of the analog cluster featuring the tachometer, oil pressure, temperature, and volts.

The Banshee's seats were fixed with lateral support mounted to the doors for easier entry and egress. The driver's seat had vertical adjustment and a cantilevered seat back that would swing forward for easier rear seat entry and egress.

1989 Stinger

Pontiac looked at the marketplace and noticed the increased interaction between small sporty vehicles, fun-to-drive outdoor vehicles, and utility types of cars. The result

Speedster interior. *John Heilig Collection*

was its 1989 dream car, the Stinger. Classified as a sport-style vehicle, the Stinger was a car with a Pontiac personality and roadability. Its aggressive exterior styling carried over to an aggressively styled interior. In addition, the Stinger was all-wheel drive for all-seasons performance.

The body of the Stinger was made up of carbon-fiber panels. The glass panels, except for the windshield, were all removable. The gray-and-green body could be transformed from two-door enclosed transportation to open-air fun, adaptable to a number of different activities. A roof light bar, adjustable rear spoiler, and removable glass roof panels completed the exterior transformation from a workday mode of transportation to weekend fun. Even the glass in the lower portion of the door could be removed and substituted with a panel containing a beverage cooler and storage box.

The Stinger was 164.8 inches long on a 98-inch wheelbase. It stood 58.8 inches tall and 73.7 inches wide. Its aggressive stance was poised on 295/55R16 Goodyear front tires and 295/55R18 Goodyear tires in the rear. Under the hood was a 3.0-liter four-cylinder 16-valve

Rageous took bold styling to a new dimension, with bulging wheel flares, ribbed sides that were a Pontiac signature, an aggressive spoiler, and a screaming red exterior to house a powerful V-8 engine. Rageous incorporated practical details as well, including a roomy rear seat with convenient accessibility, ample cargo space, and clever stowage compartments. *John Heilig*

engine that delivered 170 horsepower. The Stinger featured a three-speed automatic transmission, independent suspension, and anti-lock disc brakes. The pneumatic active suspension system allowed the vehicle to rise 4 inches higher for off-road driving.

Inside, the Stinger had seating for four adults, with additional stowage space for a variety of items. For example, the Stinger had built-in convenience items such as a pull-out radio and carrying case, a portable hand-held vacuum, electric extension cord, camper stove, hose, flashlight, picnic table, tool box, carrying case with binoculars, first aid kit, calculator, sewing kit, compass and magnifying glass, fire extinguisher, umbrella, mess kit, two small tote bags, brush, and dustpan. The rear seats could be raised 15 inches when the car was parked for a unique viewing position. All four seats could fold flat for storage and/or overnight sleeping.

1990 Sunfire

The 1990 Sunfire was a four-person subcompact sporty coupe that offered "expressive styling and aggressive performance," according to Pontiac. Powered by a 2.0-liter 16-valve DOHC turbocharged inline-four that produced 190 horsepower, the Sunfire put this power to the road through a five-speed Getrag manual transmission. Delco ABS Six anti-lock disc brakes were at all four wheels, which were shod with P225/40R19 tires in front and P225/45R20 tires in the rear. The front-wheel-drive Sunfire also had four-wheel independent suspension for excellent handling. The Sunfire was built on a 109-inch wheelbase.

Inside, the 2+2 seating offered rear seats that were angled outward for improved leg clearance, headroom, and ease of entry and exit. The front bucket seats had a six-way memory system and a fully articulated driver's seat with air-inflating lateral, lumbar, and thigh supports. In true Pontiac fashion, the steering wheel pod contained sound system and HVAC controls, a total of 13 buttons.

Sunfire was composed of carbon-fiber body panels. The doors were special two-part affairs featuring shorter, conventional front doors and two half-size rear doors, which opened from the front to rear to allow easier entry and exit. The composite headlights rotated up from the base of the windshield, which was pushed forward to just behind the front wheels.

1991 ProtoSport 4

The sixth Pontiac dream car in as many years, the ProtoSport 4 was a four-seat four-door sports car with a V-8 engine and rear-wheel drive. The ProtoSport 4 incorporated a fuchsia-tinted fluorescent "Scotch red" carbon-fiber body with

Montana Thunder was described as a crossover vehicle that was part sport utility, part minivan, and all Pontiac. Externally, the Thunder had a hood that was dominated by the signature Pontiac split grille and was accented by Ram Air hood scoops. *John Heilig*

unique fluorescent wire wheels. The steeply raked windshield was a continuation of the hood that began at the front end. The cockpit area was pushed forward on the 120-inch wheelbase to increase interior space. Pontiac's trademark highly stylized wheels also received special treatment on the ProtoSport 4. The unique 19-inch front and 20-inch rear wheels—mounted on specially designed Goodyear P225/40R19 front tires and P335/35R20 rear tires—were pushed to the outside corners to maximize interior dimensions.

"We gave the rear seat occupants of the car four more inches of legroom," said Pontiac Exterior Studio Chief John Manoogian. "Just by changing the passenger compartment and lengthening the wheelbase, we were able to create a whole new proportion for a sports car.

"The most significant feature on this car is the door mechanism," Manoogian continued. "The inspiration for these doors came from IMSA circuit race cars—the doors don't open like gull-wing doors, but curve up over the contour of the roofline of the vehicle. There is no interference with garage walls, or ceilings, or other parked cars."

From the rear, the roof area was bubbled up higher for rear-seat occupants. The roof was actually higher over the rear occupant area and depressed in the center of the car—like a wave or double bubble—to provide increased rear headroom. The ProtoSport 4 had four individual bucket seats. The two front seats had six-way power and power recline, pneumatic wings, lumbar support, thigh support, and vertical thorax support. The two individual rear bucket seats had comfort features as well, including power recline.

The headlights were of an ultra-low-profile, high-intensity-discharge (HID) system, featuring a unique ultraviolet

auxiliary headlamp system. An HID light source provided a smaller headlamp system due to the increased efficiency, approximately three to four times that of conventional incandescent light sources.

Under the hood was a 4.0-liter DOHC V-8 engine rated at 250 horsepower. It drove the rear wheels through a four-speed automatic transmission. The critical dimensions included an overall length of 192.5 inches, width of 75.7 inches at the rear fenders, and height of 50.6 inches.

1994 Sunfire Speedster

Then-Pontiac General Manager John G. Middlebrook said the Sunfire Speedster was "closer to production than any concept car we've ever produced. Traditionally, Pontiac concept cars are vehicles that are possible in the not-too-distant future," he continued. In fact, Pontiac did introduce a line of Sunfire cars in the 1995 model year.

Aiming toward younger drivers, Aztek's total length was 179 inches, while it was 77 inches wide and 67 inches tall. With the rear seats removed there was 105 cubic feet of storage space that was wide and long enough to carry the traditional 4x8 piece of plywood. Aztek featured an innovative instrument panel using Delphi Electronic Systems' Ultra-lite technology. *John Heilig Collection*

But the two-seater Sunfire Speedster was not part of that product line. In fact, the Speedster was closer to the 1990 Sunfire concept car than it was to the production car. Both concept cars featured a wide-track, ground-hugging stance with aggressively styled exteriors. "We wanted to make sure there was a definite link between the cars," said Pontiac Exterior #2 Studio Design Chief Jack Folden, "especially on the side profile and taillight shape."

Both cars had similarities under the hood as well. The 1990 car had a 190-horsepower turbocharged engine, while the 1994 car had a 2.4-liter Twin Cam 16-valve supercharged engine that delivered 225 horsepower.

The aggressive exterior flowed effortlessly into the organic interior, which featured high-gloss Sunfire Mango-painted surfaces with dark sienna and graphite leather appointments. Pontiac Interior Studio Chief Tom Grieg said, "The whole interior was designed to be as low as possible so that all of the components, tied together, would make for a very spacious looking interior. You'll be amazed by how high you feel in the car. By keeping the instrument panel low in the car, you don't have a huge mass of instrumentation in front of you and it gives you a feeling of spaciousness."

1995 300 GPX

Introduced at the 1995 North American International Auto Show in Detroit, the Pontiac 300 GPX was a preview of the next-generation Grand Prix. The 300 GPX had large wheel flares, recessed air intakes on the hood, a wide-track look, and a low roofline. Under the hood was a Ram Air

supercharged 3.8-liter V-8 that delivered more than 200 horsepower, an increase of more than 50 percent from standard. The supercharger was an Eaton Model 90 that forced 15.6 cubic meters of air per minute into the engine.

The 300 GPX also used a Torsen traction-control system that delivered torque to the wheels with the most grip. The driven axles were interconnected through a patented no-slip gearing system. The car used special Goodyear 255/40ZR18 tires mounted on aluminum wheels. The data gathered by the four anti-lock wheel sensors calculated tire pressure through tire rolling radius. When pressure varied too much a warning light appeared on the dash.

1997 Rageous

The Rageous took bold styling to a new dimension, with bulging wheel flares, ribbed sides that were a Pontiac signature, an aggressive spoiler, and a screaming red exterior to house a powerful V-8 engine. Unveiled at the North American International Auto Show in Detroit, the Rageous incorporated practical details as well, including a roomy rear seat with convenient accessibility, ample cargo space, and clever stowage compartments. Painted in a striking Red Rush, the Rageous promised power with its Ram Air hood, racy spoiler, and Rageous-specific P315/30R22 Goodyear tires.

The front of the Rageous incorporated the classic Pontiac dihedral—or "V" shape—especially in the center where the Ram Air intakes flowed downward into the aggressive lower fascia. The signature Pontiac round fog lamps were located into dihedral recesses in the lower fascia.

The rib treatments on the sides, front and rear fascias, the spoiler, and even the mirrors gave the sleek machine a rugged, protective look. The high belt line along the rear seating area was designed to give a feeling of protection without compromising visibility. Normal sport coupes are low in overall height, seat height, and ground clearance. The Rageous overcame this problem with an overall height of 55.5 inches, a front chair height of nearly 10 inches, and ground clearance of 6.4 inches. Another entry/exit problem on conventional sports coupes was that they have long, cumbersome doors and limited rear seat space. The Rageous didn't have that problem. Two 48-inch doors provided entry/exit room for the driver and front-seat passenger.

The Rageous' unique features included extra luggage carrying space. When activities called for cargo carrying, the front passenger seat and the two rear seats could fold down flat to provide extra space not available in conventional sports coupes. To access this area, the Rageous was equipped with a rear liftgate and a drop-down tailgate that eliminated liftover.

The interior had a shrink-wrap feel to it that emphasized the contours of the body and door structures. The controls were clustered around the driver in a cockpit designed to deliver information quickly. Full round gauges featured readouts in both digital and analog formats and supported the interior's cylindrical design theme. Information about the electronic or electric systems of the car was available through a reconfigurable heads-up display. A track-ball mouse on the steering wheel allowed the driver to access information such as speed, odometer reading, and outside temperature as well as control features such as the sound system, heating and ventilation, seats, cell phone, or navigation system.

A 315-horsepower V-8 engine attached to a six-speed manual transmission powered the Rageous. The critical dimensions included a wheelbase of 116.8 inches, overall length of 193.9 inches, and width of 76.4 inches at the wheel flares.

1998 Montana Thunder

A version of Pontiac's Trans Sport Montana minivan, the Montana Thunder was described by then-Pontiac General Manager Roy Roberts as "a crossover vehicle that is part sport utility, part minivan and all Pontiac."

Externally, the Montana Thunder had a hood that was dominated by the signature Pontiac split grille and accented by Ram Air hood scoops. Retractable headlamps, round fog lamps, and Thunder-specific high-mounted activity lamps at the top corners of the windshield provided lighting. The protective side cladding featured an angled rib pattern that gave the Thunder a strong appearance. The top rack was equipped with access lights for safer loading and unloading of equipment in a night setting. The rear design included a step bumper that featured an integrated flip-and-stow trailer hitch that could be deployed when needed and stowed out of sight when not in use. Another unique feature was the Thunder's integrated bike rack that was built into the rear hatch.

The interior was appointed with a futuristic feel while retrieving a favorite Pontiac performance feature from the past. The instrument pod recalled the muscle car era of the Pontiac Trans Am and Judge. Key gauges—speedometer, tachometer, voltage meter, engine temperature, fuel gauge, and oil pressure—were enclosed in a pod similar to the instrument cluster of a motorcycle. They were round and peered out of a brushed chrome faceplate.

An electronic instrument display behind the cluster pod contained an interactive reconfigurable telltale (RTT) that gave the driver real-time information about vehicle systems. The RTT featured an LCD screen and dot matrix digital display. The driver could scroll through the RTT for vehicle operating systems information via track-ball mice located at the three and nine o'clock positions on the steering wheel.

The Montana Thunder had a sporty stance reflective of classic Pontiac designs. With an overall length of 182.1 inches and a wheelbase of 112 inches, the Thunder crouched on a track width of 65.5 inches in front and 68.3 inches in the rear. The Thunder's overall width was 81 inches at the flared wheel arches and the height a chopped 65.2 inches.

1999 Aztek

Pontiac called the Aztek "an innovative crossover solution that combines the best attributes of a midsize sedan, van, and sport utility." With an aim at younger drivers, the total length was 179 inches, while it was 77 inches wide and 67 inches tall. With the rear seats removed there was 105 cubic feet of storage space that was wide and long enough to carry the traditional 4x8 piece of plywood.

Aztek featured an innovative instrument panel using Delphi Electronic Systems' Ultra-lite technology. This incorporated a thin acrylic sheet to channel light to primary display graphics. An electronic instrument display behind the cluster contained an interactive reconfigurable telltale (RTT) that gave the drive information about vehicle systems. RTT used an LCD screen and dot matrix digital display that allowed more information to be displayed. Also on the interior was a center console that slid on a track from the instrument panel to the rear seats. The overhead console had a fold-down LCD monitor for video viewing. The 10-speaker sound system had a "picnic/tailgating mode" that projected sound out the rear of the vehicle.

Aztek was front-wheel drive with traction control and rack-and-pinion steering. The tailgate folded down and had molded-in seats. There were four activity lamps integrated into the top of the liftgate to illuminate the rear of the vehicle for loading and unloading or setting up camp.

1999 GTO

In the 1960s and 1970s, the GTO was Pontiac's preeminent muscle car. The 1999 GTO concept car honored that memory. In profile, the GTO had a "Coke bottle" shape that was reminiscent of the earlier cars, while the rear quarter windows harkened back to the 1968 models. The lower body panels tapered toward the back of the doors, then flared out over the large rear wheels. Another retro feature was the hood-mounted tachometer.

The new GTO used 20-inch-diameter low-profile rear tires to put the power to the road, while there were 19-inch-diameter 40-section tires up front. The interior was composed of high-tech materials like aluminum. The center section of the dash was an extension of the hood and was color-matched to the translucent orange paint scheme with bright gold highlights.

Aztek cargo area. **John Heilig Collection**

CHAPTER 13

Others

In these days of the Big Three (or however many), it seems hard to believe that there was a time when there were hundreds of individual manufacturers. Even these manufacturers were able to create dream cars without the benefit of huge design staffs. All it took was a creative designer and the facilities to manufacture the vehicle.

Some of these vehicles were winners in their own right, though. The AMX could have been a true American sports car, were it not for the poor financial situation of American Motors. The Auburn Cabin Speedster knocked everyone's socks off when it was shown. Unfortunately, the hall where it was residing burned down and the Cabin Speedster remained only a memory until modern capabilities recreated it.

Packard had a few visions of the future, but the company's future was all too short. And the Eagle Jazz might have saved the brand, but it, too, was introduced after the brand was left for dead.

American Motors
1956 Nash Ambassador

Pinin Farina had been a design consultant to Nash from the time George Mason assumed the presidency in 1950. George Romney, who was then Nash-Kelvinator vice president—but would soon ascend to the presidency of Nash/American Motors and make a run at the presidency of the United States—was shipped to Turin to sign up Farina. The firm's design influence is evident in many Nash cars of the 1950s.

Shortly after Nash and Hudson merged to form American Motors, Farina was asked to create a new Ambassador/Hudson Hornet design for 1957. One proto-type was built and shown at the 1956 Turin Auto Show on Columbus Day, earning the car the nickname "Columbus Day Special."

The Ambassador prototype was based on a 1955 Ambassador chassis. After all, this was an exercise in body design, not mechanical design. Unlike the 1955, though, the entire length of the underbelly, with a few exceptions, was a flat pan, making it an integral part of the body.

Under the hood was the standard 253-cubic-inch Nash OHV inline-six. The only modification was to replace the downdraft carburetor with a side-draft version to lower the hood line by 6 inches. This led to a lower roofline as well.

Painted white, the Ambassador had a dark blue wool and mohair interior. Nash's (in)famous reclining seats were included, and had map pockets and ashtrays on the backs. The instrument panel was also dark blue with chrome trim around the blue-and-gold instruments.

One interesting feature was the use of "trafficators" in the B-pillars as turn signals. When the driver flipped the lever to indicate a turn, these trafficators would lift up and light.

There was one change on the car from the way it appeared in Turin and the way it came over to the United States and the way it was shown at car shows here. At Turin, the car wore simple chrome hubcaps. Later, these were changed to slotted gold wheel covers with the Pinin Farina crest in the centers.

AMX. *Daimler Chrysler Historical Collection*

Pinin Farina's Ambassador prototype was based on a 1955 Ambassador chassis. Unlike the 1955, though, the entire length of the underbelly, with a few exceptions, was a flat pan, making it an integral part of the body. Painted white, the Ambassador had a dark blue wool and mohair interior. The instrument panel was also dark blue with chrome trim around the blue-and-gold instruments. *Daimler Chrysler Historical Collection*

1969 AMX/2

American Motors could rarely be described as a forward-looking car company. Its Rambler and Ambassadors were economy cars that may well have been decades ahead of their time when they hit the roads in the 1960s, but they were not sexy, forward-looking, or adventurous.

The corporation made a serious attempt to revise its image with the Javelin, Marlin, and Matador. The Marlin was a six-seater fastback sedan that was simply too big for the style. The Javelin, thanks to Roger Penske and Mark Donohue, became the SCCA Trans-Am Challenge champion. And with the same two people working their magic, the Matador became a NASCAR winner.

In 1968, AMC decided it was time for an all-new "image car." The AMX/2 (its name was devised by Dick Teague) was chosen as a successor to the original AMX two-seater that never quite made it in the marketplace.

A competition was agreed to between Teague's AMC styling department and Giorgio Giugiaro in Italy. Giugiaro's example was carved in Styrofoam; Teague's was a complete car "beautifully detailed with an iridescent red body set off by hood vents and a rear deck lid with a flat black finish plus mock-up taillights that lit!"

Teague's design for the midengined two-seater was, of course, chosen, and it debuted at the 1969 Chicago Auto Show.

The production of the AMX/2 was planned. Teague was already completing the AMX/3, which had a flatter nose, smoother rear deck, and bigger windows. AMC was negotiating with Bizzarini in Italy and BMW in Germany for production. There were even discussions with Karmann in Germany to produce it, which would have created the AMX/K.

Auburn
1929 Cabin Speedster

This two-seater is one of the more interesting show cars, although it was originally intended for production.

The Auburn Cabin Speedster was one of the first show cars to push the influence of Charles Lindbergh's Trans-Atlantic flight. According to Michael Lamm and David Holls, in *A Century of Automotive Style,*

> The Auburn had an aluminum body without running boards, a two-place "cockpit" with wicker seats, a veed and steeply raked windshield, "periscope" backlight, cycle fenders and faired-in shock absorbers, all much like a small monoplane.

> There's some question as to who actually designed the 1929 Auburn Cabin Speedster. The design patent credits race driver Wade Morton, but it's unlikely that he had much to do with it. Alan H. Leamy, the Auburn-Cord staff designer, couldn't have done the car either, because he arrived at Auburn too late. An R. H. Robinson from Indianapolis took credit in a 1955 issue of Road & Track and it's possible that Robert Grimshaw, chief designer for Detroit's Griswold Body Co., designed the Auburn Cabin Speedster. There's no doubt that Griswold did build it.

> [It was] publicly stated that . . . the Auburn Cabin Speedster would be built in limited numbers, but [it wasn't]. The one-off Auburn Cabin Speedster, in fact, burned and melted into a puddle of aluminum during a fire that ravaged the Los Angeles auto show on Mar. 5, 1929.

DeSoto
1952 Adventurer I

This was the last of the Exner-Ghia cars. DeSoto wanted its own show car ever since Chrysler introduced the K-310. The company also had its own version of the Hemi V-8 engine and had a chassis that could handle it. The Adventurer (the I was added after Adventurer II was built) used a chassis shortened from 125 inches to 111 inches. The engine was the 276-cubic-inch, 170-horsepower DeSoto Hemi. The engine exhaust was through externally mounted pipes with finned chrome mufflers mounted under the rocker panels on each side of the car.

The Adventurer was a four-passenger touring coupe with rounded fenders and a racing-type fuel filler in the center of the rear deck. It used 16-inch wire wheels that were fully exposed through cutout wheel openings. It used a long, low hood and clean, simple lines.

Inside were four individually adjustable wing-type armchair seats. The instrument cluster was backed with satin-finished aluminum. A tachometer was included for the first time.

1954 Adventurer II

This car was designed totally at Ghia in Italy, without the assistance of then-Chrysler Styling Chief Virgil Exner. Built on a standard chassis, the Adventurer II had a plastic rear window that would retract into the trunk, allowing for some fresh air. A two-seater, the Adventurer II used the space that would have been used for rear seats to house custom luggage. The Adventurer II was built on a 125.5-inch-wheelbase chassis and was powered by a 170-horsepower V-8 engine.

Eagle
1995 Jazz

Even as Chrysler Corporation was considering the eventual demise of the Eagle division, it created the Jazz concept car for the 1995 North American Auto Show in Detroit. The Jazz was defined as "a refined representation of the future of the Eagle brand, meant to be international in character and dynamic in performance and handling characteristics." Powered by a 2.5-liter 24-valve V-6, the Jazz was also capable of performance. Neil Walling, then-director of Chrysler's International, Advanced, and Exterior Car and Minivan Design, said the Jazz took the cab-forward, wheels-to-the-corner approach and extended the windshield over the front wheels even further than other cab-forward vehicles. The rear had a dramatic direct slope to the bumper without the deck-line of a typical sedan. The wheels were "deep seated" to provide for 18-inch rubber, while the suspension was double wishbones up front and a multilink arrangement in the rear.

Inside, the driver-oriented interior was composed of shapes, rather than flowing forms. The Jazz featured a manually shiftable AutoStick automatic transmission. The rear passengers had their own HVAC and entertainment controls. Flush glass all around—including the rear window that sloped below the spoiler—enhanced visibility.

GMC
1988 Centaur

As General Motors' truck division, GMC occasionally develops dream cars to give its designers room to breathe. In 1988, the GM "Teamwork and Technology" show featured the GMC Centaur. GMC called the Centaur a "car-truck," reflecting its shape, which was more aerodynamic than other trucks of the time. The mythical centaur was half man

Adventurer was the last of the Exner-Ghia cars. It used a chassis shortened from 125 inches to 111 inches. The engine was the 276-cubic inch, 170-horsepower DeSoto Hemi. Adventurer was a four-passenger touring coupe with rounded fenders and a racing-type fuel filler in the center of the rear deck. *Daimler Chrysler Historical Collection*

and half horse, so this vehicle, which was half truck and half sedan, was aptly named.

The front half of the Centaur resembled a GM "Dustbuster" minivan, with a hood line that sloped in one continuous line from the front bumper to the cutoff for the truck bed. The Centaur had a 2,000-pound payload in its box. The box appeared longer than it really was because there was no physical cutoff between the cab and box, as in most trucks. In order to make it look shorter, GMC had an opposing color sweep line running from the top of the rear bumpers to the middle of the doors. In earlier versions of the Centaur, this section was also shaped in a "Coke-bottle" design.

Under the hood was a 3.0-liter 24-valve inline-six attached to an experimental five-speed automatic transmission. The Centaur also featured a self-leveling suspension, electric four-wheel steering, and anti-lock brakes.

Inside there was seating for five. The passenger compartment had a decided "car-like" feel to it.

Packard
1954 Gray Wolf II (Panther Daytona)

Packard revived a name from its racing past when it created the Gray Wolf II dream car in 1954. Powered by a supercharged V-8 engine, the Gray Wolf II, which was later renamed the Panther Daytona, had a fiberglass body and an interesting browlike effect over the grille. This two-seater also had small fins aft (from a 1955 update) of the rear fenders, with dual exhaust pipes exiting through the finer corners under the fins. Dick Teague created this car.

1955 Request

A later Dick Teague design for Packard, the Request, was the result of several "requests" by Packard customers seeking

Eagle Jazz. *Daimler Chrysler Historical Collection*

a return to the classic vertical grille days. According to Beverly Rae Kimes in *Packard: A History of the Motor Car and the Company*, Teague "took one of the first Four Hundred hard-tops, and had Creative Industries in Detroit accomplish the transformation. Aside from the tall grille, the Request also employed Caribbean side treatment, wire wheels and twin antennas, and a special bronze and white color scheme."

This car was eventually removed from Packard property in late 1956 and was involved in a front-end crash that ruined the grille. In 1974 a collector restored it to its original condition.

1956 Predictor

Packard's last dream car was styled by Dick Teague and built by Ghia in Turin, Italy. The Predictor shows what Packards might have looked like if the company had survived. With a front that looked like a cross between an Edsel and a Pontiac, the Predictor had a tall, vertical grille. In the rear were tailfins. It also contained seats that swiveled for easy entry and egress, as well as a sliding partial glass roof with controls overhead in the center, hidden headlights, side sculpting, a reverse-slanted rear window, and narrow-stripe whitewall tires.

Chief designer Bill Schmidt, who had come from Lincoln-Mercury, led the design team, but the car was the work of Teague. According to Beverly Rae Kimes, "The car had all the mechanical features of contemporary Packards

plus a powered 'tambour' roof, retractable headlights and a power rear window. It was primarily a styling exercise, though it was operative, for several dealers drove it, if only around the block, during its tour of the country. Literature, however, claimed the Predictor was equipped with transaxle and independent rear suspension—actually it was not.

"The Predictor was not the savior its makers hoped it would be. It was, however, very well received at the time, and today provides an interesting metal study of styling trends and a visible statement of the direction in which Packard was heading. It remained company property long after the closing of the Detroit facilities, and was later stored in a back room at Studebaker Plant No. 8 until it was deeded, with the balance of the Studebaker Automobile Collection, to the City of South Bend."

Studebaker
1950 Custom Convertible

Raymond Loewy designed this car, which was based on the standard 1950 Studebaker Custom. One unique feature was the absence of a rocker panel. In its place was a "sill line" comprised of a stainless-steel molding. Loewy also added louvers on the sides above the sill line and special door handles, and he modified the shape of the taillights.

The car was painted bronze and cream with a distinctive color separation. The upholstery was in natural leather, with deep pile floor coverings in chocolate. The convertible

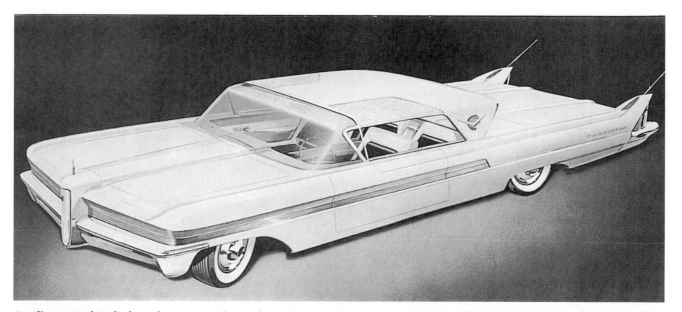

Predictor, Packard's last dream car, showed what Packards might have looked like if the company had survived. With a front that looked like a cross between an Edsel and a Pontiac, the Predictor had a tall, vertical grille. In the rear were tailfins. It also contained seats that swiveled for easy entry and egress, as well as a sliding partial glass roof with controls overhead in the center, hidden headlights, side sculpting, a reverse-slanted rear window, and narrow-stripe whitewall tires. **Daimler Chrysler Historical Collection**

top was colored light tan.

While Loewy expected many of the styling features on this car to be included in production Studebakers, only the sill line made it to the production line.

1958 Astral

Many dream cars have no method of propulsion; so much effort was expended on the design of the vehicle that none was left for the powerplant. But in almost all situations, some form of engine was designated for the vehicles. Even the Ford Nucleon had a "designated" nuclear engine, though none existed at the time or ever would. In the case of the Studebaker-Packard Astral, however, power could come from any of a number of sources, because the designers never indicated what would be used. It could have a nuclear or ionic engine and could have power beamed to it from a central source in urban areas. The Astral came from the S-P design department under the direction of Edward E. Herrmann. His goal was to give his department some experience in working with glass-reinforced plastics. "The Sputniks were launched and science fiction moved closer to reality," Herrmann said. "So we expanded our thinking."

The one-wheeled Astral looked ultra-modern, like something the Jetsons might drive. It had one enormous fin in the center of the rear, with two slanting "fender fins" that were slightly smaller. The driver sat in the normal position of this four-seater, holding two control handles that straddled the instrument panel. The panel itself featured a center bubble speedometer and six accessory gauges, all

housed in bubbles. One practical feature was the double roll bar that ran along the center spine of the car and over the rear seats.

Bibliography

Books

Hendry, Maurice. *Cadillac: The Complete History*, 4th ed. Automobile Quarterly Publications, 1983.

Kimes, Beverly Rae. *Packard: A History of the Motor Car and the Company*, 3d ed. Automobile Quarterly 1978.

Langworth, Richard and Jan Norbye. *A Complete History of the Chrysler Corporation*, Beekman House, 1985.

Magazines

Automobile Quarterly
Car Collector
Car Design
Collectible Automobile
Motor Life
Motor Trend
Road & Track
Special Interest Automobiles

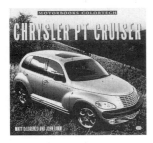

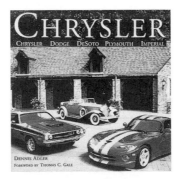